Elites, Non-Elites, and Political Realism

Elites, Non-Elites, and Political Realism

Diminishing Futures for Western Societies

John Higley

ROWMAN & LITTLEFIELD
Lanham • Boulder • New York • London

Published by Rowman & Littlefield
An imprint of The Rowman & Littlefield Publishing Group, Inc.
4501 Forbes Boulevard, Suite 200, Lanham, Maryland 20706
www.rowman.com

86-90 Paul Street, London EC2A 4NE

British Library Cataloguing in Publication Information Available

Library of Congress Cataloging-in-Publication Data
Names: Higley, John, author.
Title: Elites, non-elites, and political realism : diminishing futures for
    western societies / John Higley.
Description: Lanham, Maryland : Rowman & Littlefield, 2021. | Includes
    bibliographical references and index.
Identifiers: LCCN 2021027732 (print) | LCCN 2021027733 (ebook) | ISBN
    9781538162873 (cloth) | ISBN 9781538162880 (paperback) | ISBN
    9781538162897 (epub)
Subjects: LCSH: Power (Social sciences)—Political aspects. | Elite (Social
    sciences)—Political activity | Political realism. | Democracy. |
    Political participation.
Classification: LCC JC330 .H53 2021 (print) | LCC JC330 (ebook) | DDC
    320.01/1—dc23
LC record available at https://lccn.loc.gov/2021027732
LC ebook record available at https://lccn.loc.gov/2021027733

Contents

Acknowledgments

I owe a tremendous intellectual debt to Professor G. Lowell Field, who was my doctoral mentor at the University of Connecticut in the mid-1960s and with whom I coauthored several books and articles before Lowell's health deteriorated during the 1990s. He passed away in 1997 at the age of eighty-six, and I miss his acuity, knowledge, and friendship. Another scholar and friend who inspired me was Professor Wlodzimiez Wesolowski, the distinguished Polish sociologist who died in November 2020. Two sterling United States Foreign Service officers, Ambassador Richard Teare and Tain Tompkins (sadly deceased in 2016), were steadfast companions in work on Australian matters over many years. I am also deeply indebted to Michael G. Burton, professor emeritus of sociology at Loyola University in Maryland, and Jan Pakulski, professor emeritus of sociology at the University of Tasmania, Hobart, in Australia, for decades of fruitful collaboration and friendship. For warm collegiality over many years, I thank Zoltan Barany and Patti Maclachlan, Heinrich Best and Verona Christmas-Best, Maurizio and Raffaella Cotta, Bob and Frances Cushing, Jean-Pascal Daloz, Desley Deacon, G. William Domhoff, Fredrik Englestad, Rhonda Evans, Gary P. Freeman and Joan Yamini, Oxana Gamin-Golutvina, Trygve Gulbrandsen, Knut and Berit Grøholt, Clement Henry, Ursula Hoffmann-Lange, György Lengyel and Gabriella Ilonzski, Ian McAllister, Peter Rutland, Soňa Szomolányi, and members of the Research Committee on Political Elites of the International Political Science Association, which I had the privilege of chairing for ten years. This is the fourth volume I've published with the guidance of Susan McEachern, editorial director at Rowman & Littlefield, and I thank Susan and two anonymous reviewers for thoughtful suggestions about how to improve the book. Finally, I thank my companion, Cindy Brandimarte, for tolerating my labors, and my son, Kristian, whose love makes old age bearable.

John Higley
Austin, Texas
July 2021

Introduction

Politics are the activity in which groups who occupy a territory organize to contain many of their internal conflicts, both for their own sake and to facilitate territorial defense or expansion. But because human beings, unlike some social insects, are apparently not programmed genetically to assume different roles in society, who rises and who falls in politics is always problematic. It depends on the differing motivations and social skills of persons who act politically. All that can be said generally is that political actors constantly, if precariously, acquire some power and influence over others and are subjected to the power and influence of others.

The motivations of people who act politically are always mixed. Some are chiefly motivated by a desire for personal power and recognition. Others are more strongly motivated by a desire to nurture and aid the groups to which they belong. However, the discretion, daring, and persistence that political actions involve place a premium on essentially personal motives, whether they are conscious or not. Therefore politics tend toward forms and outcomes more consonant with the personal needs of political leaders than with what supporters and observers prefer, although leaders, of course, routinely deny such disparities.

It follows that forms of political discourse concerned with ideals are poorly suited to the analysis of what happens in politics. During modern history, however, such forms of discourse have been crushingly dominant in Western countries (principally, the Anglo-American countries and today's European Union member states plus Norway, Switzerland, and Iceland; see Huntington 1996, 47–53, 157–63). During the eighteenth and nineteenth centuries, a series of ideologies, or worldviews, evolved in them, and it became culturally necessary to discuss and analyze politics in terms of those ideologies. None dealt seriously with the mixture of motives that propel political action, least of all the importance and prevalence of personal motives. Instead each posited a distinctive assumption about human motivation in general and posited the kind of political outcome that would supposedly satisfy a population so motivated. Although numerous specific viewpoints and doctrines emerged from the ideologies, it is sufficient here to distinguish three abstract positions.

The first position, conservatism, derived from premodern societies but retained many adherents until well into the nineteenth century. It presumed that social order is in some sense natural and hence basically satisfactory to all people. Certain hierarchies of power and privilege are likewise natural, perhaps even divinely ordained. Where a society respects and organizes itself along these hierarchies, persons in its upper reaches will be motivated to command well and those below to obey effectively.

The second position was generalized liberalism. Originating in the political and social upheavals of the seventeenth century, liberalism formed the basis for diverse republican, democratic, and other reformist viewpoints by the nineteenth century. It presumed that successful social functioning depends on giving people reasonable opportunities and sufficient incentives to follow their self-interest. In the political realm, this meant repudiating the governmental controls that independent and self-reliant citizens resented, specifically by leaving most economic matters to be regulated through competition in markets.

During the nineteenth century, a third position, socialism, developed. It presumed that human selfishness is excessive if uncontrolled and that when opportunities for self-aggrandizement are severely limited, somewhat altruistic social and communal motivations can be relied on in the operations of society. In its original form, socialism called for various statist and cooperative schemes to handle economic production and distribution. Later it urged assorted public measures that would distribute incomes and risks more equitably.

It is important to note that each of the three positions (and this was true of Western thought in general during the modern period) purported to speak for all persons. It was never denied, of course, that at a given moment many misguided individuals might adhere to positions other than the one being espoused. But such waywardness was thought to be somehow remediable. Conservatives, liberals, and socialists alike presumed that with sufficient leadership efforts all, or nearly all, people would become conservatives or liberals or socialists. This presumption was a fundamental misconception of politics. The interests that give rise to different allegiances and conflicts between them are not subject to reconciliations in the sense that everyone will ultimately accept one specific position or outcome as just. Instead political actions secure wide assent only when persons and groups who oppose each other make expedient judgments that a specific position or policy outcome is acceptable in the absence of any better possibility.

Thus, in a modern, highly productive country with a long record of peaceful succession to political office, such as the United States or Britain, political functioning depends on the fact that a great many groups whose circumstances are diverse do not demand outcomes fully consonant with their conscious self-interests. All but tiny fractions of poor and otherwise disadvantaged Americans and Britons tolerate what they view as inadequate government provisions for their support. Apart from ugly racial or ethnic confrontations and occasional hooliganism at sporting events and music concerts, they do not engage in highly disruptive riots and demonstrations because they judge that such actions would probably prove ineffective, dangerous, and therefore inexpedient. Similarly, many middle-class Americans and Britons believe that government welfare programs subsidize laziness and deprive society of cheap and economically beneficial labor. But by and large, they tolerate these welfare programs, and when even very conservative politicians refrain from dismantling them, they recognize the inaction as expedient. The politicians presumably fear that drastically cutting welfare benefits might provoke dissident behavior hard to control. Still sharper conflicts occur over other matters, but these too are contained by judgments of what is expedient. For example, many poor Americans and Britons believe that the rich should pay most taxes, while the rich usually judge themselves overtaxed. Yet few persons on either side carry their strong feelings about taxation beyond voting for vaguely "liberal" or vaguely "conservative" politicians.

The way in which political positions and outcomes are based on considerations of expediency is even more evident in countries that have lacked stable representative political institutions. In them, institutions do little to restrain people from pursuing their self-interest more or less fully. Because there is no tradition that presumes a common interest and portrays ballot box decisions as legitimate, whatever civil peace exists over time clearly reflects the conscious, expediential decisions of opposing groups to settle for outcomes that are highly unsatisfactory but are, for the moment, the best that are available.

Consider a country like Argentina. There organized labor and other populist groupings were for decades committed to a political movement associated with the name of ex-president Juan Perón. Generally better-off, propertied parts of the population meanwhile supported several traditional parties, at least when electoral politics were temporarily practiced. However, both camps largely deferred to military juntas that recurrently ruled the country by simple force. The deeply divided segments of Argentine society regularly judged that acquiescing in military rule was the best option available. A dramatic exception was the guerrilla uprising by a number of left-wing idealists, the Montoneros, during the 1970s. By refusing to accept a situation that was far from what they considered to be ideal, the Montoneros succeeded only in bringing about their own extermination at the hands of the military.

The point is that in the United States, Britain, and Argentina there is nothing like a general, detailed consensus about political actions and outcomes. In all three, public policies directly restrict the interests of most persons and are consequently seen as unjust. In all three, the central question is: How much does one resist and how much does one acquiesce? In the United States and Britain, decisions to acquiesce are greatly aided by traditions of representative government and the accompanying belief that one has some chance of altering government policy by argument. Lacking a comparable tradition and belief, Argentines can only acquiesce on the less palatable ground that if they do not then everyone will be destroyed by everyone else's self-assertions. But in the United States, Britain, Argentina, or any other relatively large and complex society, the continuation or overthrow of governments as well as the success of specific policies depends on the amounts of acquiescence or resistance that large numbers of people judge to be expedient.

This amounts to saying that an objective, realistic view of politics is incompatible with the ideologies that shaped Western political discourse during recent centuries. Politics are never more than the ways participants in broad conflicts organize to manage those conflicts. Political realism involves assessing the current organization of power within areas of conflict, the motivations and resources of the conflicting persons and groups, and the motivations, skills, and options of those who are in positions from which issues in conflicts can be manipulated. By disregarding such considerations, ideologies have no explanatory truth. Nor do they have any moral truth for persons other than those who accept a particular ideology's assumption about human motivation and do not care how well or poorly the policies that flow from it suit other people.

This denies the basic premise on which the prevailing conception of politics rests, which is that the great differentiation of statuses and interests in a complex society like the United States or Britain is nevertheless compatible with adherence to a single set of ideals and goals—that what is good for one is still somehow good for all. This book presumes, instead, that self-interest motivates most political action, that political outcomes are shaped by the judgments of self-interested persons and groups as to what claims and actions are and are not expedient, and that, in the final analysis, it is only the efforts of somewhat more broadly oriented leaders—political elites—to manage and limit conflicts and prevent a war of all against all.

The disarray that currently afflicts the United States, Britain, and other Western countries is rooted in the reluctance of many educated persons to entertain these distasteful assumptions about politics. They are unwilling to acknowledge that politics arise out of, and only out of, rationally irreconcilable conflicts of interest among people. Conflicts are rationally irreconcilable in the sense that parties to them cannot be shown or persuaded that they are mistaken about their interests. Not all conflicts have this character, of course, but many do, and it is these that are the bases of politics.

Where conflicts of interest are not rationally reconcilable, politics are the alternative to civil warfare. As history readily shows, politics are hardly a reliable alternative, yet they are grudgingly accepted. This is because the many people in any society who lack substantial self-confidence, ambition, and assertiveness are usually prepared to tolerate politics to reduce the amount of violence and disorder that would otherwise occur. They are prepared to put up with political actions unsatisfactory to themselves to achieve a semblance of peace. Behind any smoothly functioning political system, in other words, are expediential and tacit conclusions by individuals and groups trying to claim that all they think they deserve is unprofitable and that conforming to the political organization and distribution of privilege that happen to exist offers a better return than they might obtain by openly challenging the established order.

This implies that political actions never fully "solve" social problems in any objective moral sense. "Social justice" is never attained through politics (nor through any other activity) because, in assuming that differences of interest are ultimately mistaken, social justice is an empty concept. Political actions result only in *settlements* that contain, discourage, or repress the expression of interests that are not, and for the most part could not be, fully satisfied. Although settlements usually involve fairly even-handed compromises between conflicting groups, they necessarily sacrifice some interests that happen not to be well represented at the points and places where settlements are reached. One reason is that elite persons who are in positions to shape settlements normally expect to gain something for themselves and their friends from their actions. In any settlement, some interests are sacrificed merely by elites' efforts to ensure that they, at least, are not disadvantaged by it.

Because there are no strictly objective solutions to many conflicts of interest, and because elite persons who make their weight
felt when shaping political settlements regularly produce more
advantages for themselves and their allies than for others, elites are
commonly thought to be immoral, callous, and deceitful. From perspectives that would be appropriate when judging many nonpolitical
actions, they are. But as a generalization about most or all elites,
this common judgment is erroneous because politics are a necessary
activity that never allows fully open and trusting behavior. Political
actions that are naïvely open and trusting are normally ineffective,
while actions that do not seek to coerce some persons in ways that
are advantageous to others are not political.

Given this nature of politics per se, the moral judgments properly
appropriate to politics and elites are complex, subtle, and controversial. They are concerned with effectiveness, with humaneness,
and with culturally shaped notions of fairness. Basically, they are
concerned with the obligation of elites to avoid practices that unnecessarily reduce the satisfactions of some persons or unnecessarily
degrade some persons' attitudes and behavior. Yet what constitute
unnecessarily harsh political actions by elites is disputable. For
example, elites of a liberal persuasion tend to approve of political
practices that create or preserve a certain type of self-reliant person.
Elites who think of themselves as socialists endorse practices that
foster a more altruistic kind of person. This means that liberal and
socialist elite factions tend to disagree about what constitute unnecessarily harsh and degrading political actions.

The social function of politics is to make the existence of all larger
territorial organizations of people possible. These range from city-
states to modern national states to far-reaching empires to weakly
organized supranational entities such as the European Union or
the United Nations. But when politics successfully perform this
function by suppressing overt conflict and producing a reliability
of expectations in social life, they tend to conceal their own nature
from persons who benefit most from successful politics. Secure and
influential, they lose sight of the basis, nature, and function of politics, and they come to mistake their own situations and sensibilities
for those of people in general. They find it impossible to accept that

political institutions and processes that so effectively protect and nurture them are regarded as more or less iniquitous by less fortunate people in their own and other societies.

In this way, successful politics undermine their own basis. The most favored social strata and categories come to contain larger and larger numbers of sentimental and unrealistic persons who are unwilling to recognize that their fortunate circumstances emanate in large measure from how elites in their societies practice politics. They like to talk about such things as politics without coercion, conflict resolution, participatory democracy, fruitful "conversations" between persons and groups who disagree, and other constructs that can only be mainly imaginary. They seek to impose respect for such constructs on elites who need their support.

Yet if elites start to believe and profess such naïveté seriously, their effectiveness is crippled. In the eyes of less advantaged people at home and abroad, such professions are patently insincere, and elites who voice them are contemptible. Only a ruthless tradition of intellectual honesty or a protected private tradition of objectivity among elites and their immediate supporters can resist the tendency of successful politics to undermine their own basis. Bolstered by their global dominance, politics in Western liberal countries in about 1900 were perhaps the most successful politics ever practiced. Yet the intellectual life of none of these countries was able to prevent the naïve moral claims that successful politics inspired from coming to pervade the thoughts and utterances of many otherwise sophisticated citizens. As a contribution to political realism in the twenty-first century, this book tries to counter such prevalent but delusive outlooks.

The aim of chapter 1, "Elites, Non-Elites, and Politics," is a broad and realistic understanding of what is and is not possible in politics. Main variations in the political behaviors of elites are interrelated with main changes in the political orientations of non-elites during modern history down to the present. Circumstances in which variations in elite political behavior occur and their consequences for political stability and instability are specified. The political orientations of non-elite populations in preindustrial, industrial, and postindustrial settings and limits they impose on elite action are likewise specified. The predominance of elites or non-elites in different stages of economic and political development is shown to shape what occurs politically.

Chapter 2, "Elites, Non-Elites, and Revolution," draws on chapter 1 to analyze the origins, processes, and consequences of revolution. Although firm generalizations are hindered by the contingent circumstances from which revolution springs, there is little doubt that it seldom, if ever, results in political improvement. While much is heard from persons outraged by what they regard as fundamental deficiencies in today's regimes, not least Western democracies, the sweeping "revolutionary" changes that some of these persons demand lie well beyond the limits of politics and are, from the standpoint of political realism, dreams and deeply imprudent wishes.

Chapter 3, "Elites, Non-Elites, and Democracy," also draws on chapter 1 to consider the spread of democracy during the past two centuries and how powerful populist leaders today, exemplified by Donald Trump in the United States, Boris Johnson in Britain, Viktor Orbán in Hungary, and Jaroslaw Kaczynski in Poland, injure democracy by exploiting insecurities that have become widespread among non-elites. Professing to believe that a society characterized by at least a rough equality in political life is possible, populist leaders like these are residual bearers of the utopianism so prominent in Western political thought during modern history.

Chapter 4, "Ultimate and Instrumental Values in Liberal Democracy," tries to show how liberal democracy can be put on a firmer intellectual and comparative footing than recent political thought has recognized. As a concept and phenomenon, liberal democracy conflates ultimate liberal and instrumental democratic values. The ultimate liberal value—a social milieu in which persons are free and equal in active political and social roles—should be distinguished from the instrumental value of democracy, which depends fundamentally on the kind of politics practiced by elites.

Chapter 5, "The Arab Spring Folly," applies generalizations in chapter 1 to well-established patterns of elite and non-elite behavior in Egypt, Libya, Syria, and Tunisia before, during, and since the Arab Spring in 2011. Afghanistan since 2001 and Iraq since 2003 are also examined. Paying insufficient attention to deeply embedded elite and non-elite patterns of political behavior made U.S. and

European efforts to implant democracy in these countries destined to fail.

Chapter 6, "Political Realism in the Twenty-First Century," argues that to counter proliferating and dire foreign and domestic threats to the United States and all other Western countries, elites have no realistic alternative to a concerted, if unspoken, holding operation between now and mid-century. The chapter asks what this may entail and whether it is feasible.

An epilogue, "The American Preoccupation with Non-Elites," observes that at no time down to the present has American political thought been hospitable to frank expressions of the idea that objective features of modern society, such as the inescapable importance of elites, forever impede the attainment of populistic goals. Instead questionable assumptions about the causal importance of non-elites in politics have underlaid and driven American political thought.

Chapter One

Elites, Non-Elites, and Politics

Attempts to generalize about politics have been based on two different principles. One is that politics reflect and are driven by broad social forces; the other presumes that politics are substantially independent of such forces. The first principle, which is sometimes labeled the sociology of politics, assigns causal primacy to the interest positions and dispositions of all social actors relative to each other. The second principle, which has underlain political science, holds that those who are politically influential require separate analysis and understanding because they operate within latitudes of choice and action that are usually quite wide. The first principle focuses on social differentiation in the tradition of Marx, the second on political hierarchy in the tradition of Pareto. The first is concerned predominantly with the political behavior of non-elites; the second predominantly with that of elites. This chapter seeks to combine the two traditions.

The chapter's generalizations about politics are deductive and rationalistic; they purport, most simply, to "make sense." Roles played by elites, that is, the small number of especially influential persons in a society, are contrasted with those played by non-elites, that is, the bulk of a society's adult population. The generalizations deal with all societies, although emphasis is on the experiences of Western societies during the modern historical period to the present. The generalizations must of course be judged according to observed or recorded realities. Have events occurred as they would if they were true? Do they make better sense of political continuities and changes than others? If they do, are there nevertheless clear and undoubted facts that show them to be at least in part mistaken?

These are questions that a reader must, in the end, answer for her- or himself. "Can the generalizations be proved empirically?" is not, however, a fair question. No seriously explicative scheme, even in the most experimental and reputedly scientific fields, can meet such a test. The internal structure of the physicist's atom is not observable and empirically provable. Things that *are* observable happen as they would if generalizations about them were true and there is no better or simpler explanation.

ELITES AND POLITICS

Propositions about elites being a feature of all societies have often been rooted in observations of superior individual endowments, be they of intelligence or energy, talent, or personal magnetism. So long as such disparities exist, it has been asserted, so long will there be elites. This was the general view of the ancients, transmitted to us primarily by Aristotle. It has been sharply opposed by many democrats and social radicals who have sought to demonstrate that elites are not those with superior endowments but merely persons and groups who are economically and socially advantaged in power competitions. This view pervades the modern liberal democratic and socialist traditions. Activists in these traditions contend that the existence of elites can be terminated either by removing the economic and social advantages that some persons and groups enjoy or by abolishing power concentrations that spur competitions among them—remedies that often go together. There are no historical instances, however, where such remedies have been successfully applied in large populations for significant lengths of time.

Individual endowments as well as social advantages are undoubtedly important when studying elite recruitment and composition. But to dispense with either or both (in a thoroughly equitable society, for example) would not eliminate elites. This is because they derive from a more fundamental and universal fact of social life, namely, the absence in any large collectivity of a common interest that extends to detailed features of organization and policy. While it is true that most collectivities rest on a base of broad social and cultural understandings, these understandings tend to be ambiguous and rough. They do not prevent people from claiming statuses and other valued items for themselves, their kin, friends, and allies that others do not accept as fully legitimate. Acceding to such claims is often as much a matter of judging that it is inexpedient to resist them as it is of recognizing that the persons and groups making them have some culturally or socially defined right to do so. In broad arenas of social action, common interest is minimal and must always be supplemented by authoritative decisions that dissenters and opponents dare not or find it inexpedient to resist.

Common interest is even more limited as regards detailed aspects of organizational functioning. The operations of any relatively complex and sizable organization involve day-to-day allocations and reallocations of tasks and, therefore, of organizational statuses. Merely for such organizations to survive, not to mention grow and prosper, "intelligent" and "objective" decisions that transcend individual interests must constantly be made. However, there can seldom be any firm consensus among all organizational members about the rightness of such decisions. This is partly because only a few persons are in positions that afford a relatively comprehensive view of the organizational effort and its present location in time and space relative to its goals. Yet such a view is usually necessary to have a firm opinion about decisions that are needed. Equally important, the necessity for constant decision making deprives the mass of an organization's members of the time they would need to work out how organizational interests apply to current problems and needs. Even a relatively unimportant decision changes the lineup of influence for the next decision, so the details of an organization's structure and needs are always different today from what they were yesterday. This means that any incipient consensus among organizational members inevitably focuses on yesterday's structure and needs.

The absence of a common interest or understanding that extends to detailed features of organization and policy means that the structures and processes of organizations are *arbitrary* in character. They are created and modified by the decisions of those who happen to be in strategic locations at any moment. But whether their decisions are right or wrong can never be demonstrated convincingly to all those affected by them. Like human beings in general, strategic decision makers in organizations sometimes act selfishly, sometimes capriciously, and sometimes with altruistic intent. All that is certain is the basically arbitrary character of their decisions from the standpoint of other organizational members. There is no way for decisions to be made and for organizations to be effective other than having some person or persons decide what is to be done.

Recognition of these prosaic facts about organization gives to elites their importance in political and social matters. Organizations of any size or complexity always involve arbitrary decision making by persons who happen to be strategically placed in them. If we call these persons "elites," we can say that large and complex organization necessarily creates them. In this sense only are elites an inherent feature of any larger collectivity or society. All other philosophical underpinnings for the existence of elites are less persuasive and more debatable.

Recognizing this is not, however, to paraphrase Robert Michels's dictum that "who says organization says oligarchy" (1915/1962, 365) because oligarchies, polyarchies, power elites, establishments, or other euphemisms for strategically placed persons in organizations impute specific structural and processual characteristics (Winters 2011). Apart from statements about their small number and greater social and psychic rewards that persons who command organizations presumably enjoy, there is no way in which one can derive statements about other properties of elites from the dynamics of organizations. Whether elites are cohesive, closed, cooptative, conspiratorial, and so on are questions answerable only through empirical investigation. Although elites are the inescapable consequence of complex organization, their detailed features vary according to circumstances.

These considerations dictate that a technical definition of elites be minimal. It is sufficient if it refers to strategic placement in an arbitrarily organized (that is, nonconsensual) social universe. In the abstract, *elites are those persons with power to affect organizational outcomes individually, regularly, and seriously.* Power is the ability to make offers and threats that are likely to alter the motivations of persons other than the power wielder. Although there is apparently no way in which power can be observed directly and measured accurately, it is plausible to assume that it normally inheres in the uppermost positions of organizations.

Generalizations about elites in politics are therefore focused on the behavior of persons occupying strategic positions in large and complex organizations, including governments and hierarchically structured social and political movements, and what their behavior means for other social categories and phenomena. It is left to the analyst to specify the organizational setting in which elites are located and those aspects of their behavior to be examined. This book is concerned with the political behavior of *national elites*, that is, persons with power to affect political outcomes at the macro level of organized societies individually, regularly, and seriously.

Put differently, the interest here is in persons who have power sufficient to influence or upset, regularly and seriously, the determination of national policies. The stipulation of "regularity" means that, at a minimum, the person's point of view and possible actions regarding specific decisions are consistently seen by other persons as significant factors in the making of those decisions, although this does not mean that an elite person is an active participant in each policy decision (Merritt 1970, 105). The stipulation that the person can act "seriously" in this regard means that, as Suzanne Keller phrased it, her or his "judgments, decisions, and actions have important and determinable consequences for many members of society" (1963, 20).

To put it still another way, national elites consist of those who are capable, if they wish, of making substantial political trouble for persons who happen to be incumbents of authoritative positions without being promptly repressed. In this sense, national elites contain not only prestigious, relatively "established" leaders—recognized politicians, important businessmen, high-level civil servants, senior military officers—but also, in varying degrees in different societies, relatively transitory and less individually known leaders of mass organizations such as trade unions, churches, and other important voluntary associations and social movements. This subsumes persons and groups often labeled "counter-elites" because they quite clearly have the power, although perhaps mainly through negation, to affect political outcomes regularly and seriously. It will be seen subsequently that this aspect of the definition is fundamental to a classification that can be used to explain certain recurring relationships among political phenomena in terms of elite behavior and motivation.

There is no denying that elites constitute a somewhat elastic category, yet they can be more readily identified and demarcated than categories such as ruling classes, political classes, charter groups, establishments, opinion makers, or "leaders." In his book *Coming Apart: The State of White America, 1960–2010*, Charles Murray estimates that "those who have risen to jobs that directly affect the nation's culture, economy, and politics . . . [number] . . . fewer than a hundred thousand people and perhaps only ten thousand or so" (2012, 17–18). Thomas R. Dye, the author of *Who's Running America?* counts "top positions in the institutional structure of American society as slightly more than 4,000" (2014, 11). Through interviews he conducted personally with 550 top-ranking position holders in the United States, including two former presidents, Michael Lindsay identified "a complex network of power involving individuals, institutions, and organizational fields that ultimately reaches across the country and around the globe. It is through this matrix that decisions of national and international consequence are made, elite newcomers are assimilated, and resources of all kinds—political, economic, social, and cultural—are distributed. In essence, this is how power operates [in the United States]" (2014, 4–5).

Using organizational-positional identifications of elites supplemented by studies of the interaction networks of key decision makers in different organizations and societal sectors, researchers have estimated that the number of elite persons at the national level is perhaps five thousand in France (Dogan 2003) and Germany (Bürklin and Rebenstorf 1997) and around two thousand in Norway (Gulbrandsen et al. 2002) and Denmark (Monck, Möller, and Togeby 2001). The elite that presides over the European Union and Eurozone is estimated to consist of 600 to 650 persons, many of who simultaneously hold top decision-making positions in their home countries (Cotta 2014). It is important to underscore that these are *political* specifications of national (and the European Union's supranational) elites; they do not include, as Peter Turchin does in his thesis about "elite overproduction" in contemporary America, the several million persons who hold elevated business, wealthy, professional, educational, and assorted media and cultural statuses (2016, 75–98).

Three stipulations are necessary. First, a dichotomy consisting of elites and non-elites obviously oversimplifies and distorts the actual political stratification of societies. In this book, nonetheless, all those who have power to affect political outcomes individually, regularly, and seriously at a polity's macro-level comprise elites, and all others are non-elites. The license for this apparent recklessness lies in the explicative and predictive payoffs that build on it. Second, "elite" will be used in its plural form—"elites"—because there are always in organized societies important differences between elite persons and factions. Third, to relieve the tedium deriving from constant use of "elites," synonyms such as "the powerful" or "the influential" will sometimes be employed, but these are stylistic variations that always refer to elites as defined here.

ELITE DISUNITY AND POLITICAL INSTABILITY

The presence or absence of stability is one of the major differences in the functioning of political systems that can be explained because of certain historically determined differences in elite behavior. It is unusual for political power to be effectively institutionalized, as it has been for many generations in Britain, the United States, the Netherlands, Sweden, Canada, Australia, New Zealand, and a few other countries. Stability is marked by the *absence* of obviously irregular seizures of executive power or obvious interference in policymaking by the military through threats of forcible intervention. Every four years since 1789, a president has taken office in the United States because of election and served out a term, unless dying or resigning, as the effective head of the American political system. In Britain over an even longer time span, prime ministers and cabinets have regularly succeeded each other as the chief political authority in accordance with mostly informal principles and rules that are well known and respected.

The personalized manipulation of political institutions through individual and direct control of the military has been, and is, much more common. Typically, there is a distinct elite faction that effectively commands organized coercive forces and is willing to arbitrate political decisions no matter what existing institutions prescribe. It is of little consequence analytically whether this faction centers on a traditional monarch, a civilian coalition tied to professional military commanders, or is an overt military junta. What is consequential is that elites, no matter what their partisan inclinations may be, see government power as personalized and directly dependent on the support of organized coercive forces. Elite persons and groups critical of current societal organization, for whatever reason, necessarily view change in terms of removing or altering the persons and groups that effectively control those forces. In their eyes and in the eyes of their opponents, power flows not from the incumbency of institutional positions but from the success of a specific person or group in gaining at least temporary control over the principal means of coercion. Elite members, fearing power plays by other members, distrust each other and are inclined to fight fire with fire. Attempts to seize power by force are seen by all as plausible, even probable, eventualities.

This is the basic aspect of *disunified elites*. Where they exist, government power oscillates between "democratic" and "dictatorial" poles. The oscillations are transitory and circumstantial manifestations of elite disunity and the political system's inherent instability. For reasons that will later be made clear, neither democratic nor dictatorial arrangements can by themselves unite disunified elites and stabilize institutions. Instability is the *permanent* character of a political system so long as elite persons and groups hold the view that, no matter its current complexion, the hold on government power is subject to sharp and sudden changes. Such perceptions and expectations are evidence, *prima facie*, of disunified elites.

Disunified elites and unstable institutions are easily discerned in the histories and contemporary situations of the great majority of independent national states. For example, a deep dichotomy between monarchical and bourgeois factions characterized French elites for many decades before and after the revolution. The dichotomy developed into a three-way struggle between right-wing, centrist, and left-wing factions during the latter part of the nineteenth century. Because of elite disunity, French political institutions were for more than two centuries beset by actual or threatened seizures of power by force. Such seizures resulted in the establishment of France's two empires and three of its five republics. A fourth republic arose from the invasion of France by liberating military forces near the end of World War II, and the present Fifth Republic originated in 1958 as the result of a threatened military rebellion.

From the early nineteenth century elites in Spain exhibited similar evidence of disunity. During most of that century power passed between liberal and conservative elite factions because of military coups. After a precarious monarchical interlude that began in 1875, coups and uprisings during the 1920s and 1930s produced the Primo de Rivera dictatorship, a republic, a blood-soaked civil war, and the Franco dictatorship. Especially apparent during the years surrounding World War I, disunity characterized German elites from unification of the nation in 1870 until the Nazi consolidation of power in 1933–1934. A similar disunity of Italian elites after national unification in 1861 led to political instability that bordered on civil war in 1921–1922, military arbitration, and creation of a fascist regime by 1926. These and other European patterns of elite disunity and political instability (in Greece and Portugal, for example) were like most Latin American, Middle Eastern, and Southeast Asian patterns after cessations of colonial rule.

Historical evidence thus indicates that politics normally approximate lethal struggles by mutually mistrusting elite persons and groups seeking to defend or advance partisan interests with little regard for propriety or cost. Occasionally, to be sure, a set of political institutions may be maintained, accidentally, for several decades (usually in monarchical or dictatorial but sometimes in republican or "democratic" form), but in such cases there is little reason for elites to count on stability.

ELITE UNITY AND POLITICAL STABILITY

Of supreme interest in political analysis, therefore, are those comparatively few societies in which instability has *not* been the order of the day. For as noted, a few societies have displayed patterns of institutionalized authority and procedure that have been respected and perpetuated over long periods. In them, irregular seizures of executive power by force have been unknown and considered implausible by most influential participants in politics. These deviant cases are explicable *only* in terms of elite behavior. The historically normal situation of political instability has been abrogated only where elites have become unified.

It is worth making the rationale for this claim clear. The stability of large polities is never the result of all social actors cooperating voluntarily, peacefully, and with adequate information. It is always the artificial product of shrewd decisions made by those who are influential and politically active. In essence, this shrewdness consists of suppressing, distorting, or otherwise manipulating issues that, if expressed and acted on openly and widely, would result in disastrous conflict. Shrewdness in making decisions that affect large social categories requires that elite members trust each other not to expose their respective stratagems. It implies almost conspiratorial behavior among numerous decision makers and other political actors. They must agree about the desirability of a stable political system, usually in something like its current form, and about the goals, if any, toward which the system is ostensibly moving. Political stability requires elites that are unified in this sense.

There are, however, two markedly different kinds of unified elites that are reflected in two substantially different kinds of political stability. One kind, an *ideological unified elite*, is marked by the uniform profession of a single and defined ideology by all or nearly all elite persons. Unity is manifested in the refusal of these persons to take clashing positions publicly on current policies or political beliefs. Instead near unanimity is expressed by those who are in positions of power and influence. The image of a single, homogenous leadership group is assiduously fostered by those who currently hold power as well as by those aspiring to hold it.

The apparent unanimity that marks this kind of elite arises from the determination of uppermost leaders, imbued with a specific ideology, to afford no opening for the intrusion of unsound outsiders into policymaking. Behind the public profession of complete agreement about current policies and goals—behind the uniform expression of a single and defined ideology—there exists an apparatus of power sufficient to force all or most current and aspiring elite persons to harmonize their public statements with views that are currently orthodox. Defining what is orthodox is the task of a few individuals in the highest elite positions. Adherence to the orthodoxy obviously blocks the expression of divergent interests.

Content of the ideology that members of the elite profess is of little analytical importance. It must be sufficiently diffuse and removed from present conditions to permit flexibility in interpreting current but always changing realities. Probably it must be focused on some imaginary social condition toward which the society is claimed to be moving and not on conditions directly within the reach of policies. In a word, the ideology must be utopian. But whether it describes a future classless society or a radically superior society in which eternal salvation or pastoral contentment for all will exist is of little consequence for the kind of unity that prevails among the elite. It is sufficient if substantial conformance to a generalized ideological position blocks the emergence of persons and factions with conflicting interests and opinions.

Because the only permissible public position that seeks to organize societal endeavors is defined and monopolized by those already in power, political institutions can be centralized and stabilized to a degree unknown elsewhere. Individuals and factions who want to alter those institutions can be identified readily, and they possess few means with which to appeal for non-elite support. Unless defeated in international warfare, historical evidence indicates that, once established, institutions operated by an ideological unified elite are stable for long periods.

The other kind of unified elite, a *consensual unified elite*, does not involve all or most elite persons taking the same political position in public. There is no enforced and single ideology to which all or most elite persons adhere; instead persons and groups with power and influence take clearly divergent positions on matters of public discussion. Their positions often accord with opposing ideologies, as in the century-long conflict between conservatives and liberals in the British and Swedish elites of the nineteenth century and in the subsequent conflict between liberals and socialists in the same elites during the first half of the twentieth century.

The striking aspect of such conflicts is that they occur within a tradition of political contest, that is, under rules that are nowhere comprehensively codified but are widely understood to remove serious personal danger from political contests. The rules and their observance emanate from a structuring of power in which most elite members have sufficient personal access to policy decision making so that it is in their interests to avoid seriously disruptive actions and keep politics manageable. Although elite members and factions disagree and oppose each other in limited political struggles, power is distributed so that all or most can have an impact on outcomes sufficient to deter them from translating their struggles into attempts to seize power by force. Political institutions are, accordingly, stable so long as the elite consensus and implicit rules underlying it persist.

As chapter 2 discusses, an ideological unified elite originates in revolutionary circumstances that enable a movement dogmatically professing some utopian ideology to suppress and supplant previously existing elites (as in Russia, Germany, Italy, and Iran during the twentieth century). It may also originate through imposition by military conquest or hegemony (as in China or Eastern Europe following World War II). By contrast, a consensual unified elite originates in changes of situation and attitudes in a disunified elite whose members for the most part continue in elite status.

The consensual unification of a disunified elite takes at least two distinct forms. Neither is a protracted process, and each can be quite closely dated as a historical event. One form is an *elite settlement* in which opposing persons and factions manage to bring major disputes to a close and establish a basis for mutual trust. The other form is a possible accompaniment of a country attaining independence from foreign rule whereby local native-born elites take over after the usually forced withdrawal of foreign rulers and find themselves substantially harmonious and trusting.

The first historical instance of an elite settlement occurred in England's "Glorious Revolution" of 1688–1689, and it is worth recalling its main features briefly (Burton and Higley 1987). The English elite had long been bitterly and deeply disunified, as was particularly evident in the Civil Wars and Interregnum between 1642 and 1660. In 1660, the monarchical system was restored, albeit with some shifting of positions and blurring of lines between elite factions. One main faction, the Tories, sought to exploit their association with royalism, while another, the Whigs, maintained a vague but definite association with the non-elite forces that had been antimonarchical during and after the Civil Wars.

The Tory monarchical faction became thoroughly identified with the religious position and institutional features of the governmentally established Church of England. But when, in 1685, the birth of a son to James II, who professed both Roman Catholicism and an absolutist version of monarchical power, made an indefinite Catholic succession to the throne likely, the Tory faction was as discomfited as its rival, the Whigs. Principal leaders of the two factions, fearing a resumption of civil war, joined in inviting the military intervention of William of Orange from Holland and eventually made him king (and Mary, his Anglo-Scottish consort, queen) under terms that effectively guaranteed the joint preeminence of the two previously rival factions.

Occurring in a predominantly agrarian society in which elites were necessarily small and exclusive, those events marked the beginning of the tradition of limited political contest under known and respected but largely uncodified rules that has characterized British elites ever since (see Plumb 1967 and Barone 2007 for similar interpretations). In her masterful history of constitutionalism, Linda Colley attributes Britain's lack of a written constitution most directly to "a precocious entrenchment of the powers and position of the Westminster Parliament" in the Glorious Revolution, although the extent of its powers has been a perennial subject of debate ever since (Colley 2021, 215).

An analogous sudden and basic elite settlement occurred in Sweden's five-week constitutional settlement of 1809 after a century of infighting between "Hat" and "Cap" factions that involved a coup d'état against parliament in 1772 and a military officer's mortal wounding of King Gustav III at a masked ball in 1792 (Rustow 1970). Somewhat less clearly, an elite settlement appeared to occur in Mexico during 1928–1929 when intricate political maneuvers by the president, Plutarco Calles, led to an omnibus party, eventually known as the PRI, that operated a stable presidential system after a long experience of bloody turmoil (Knight 1992).

An important recent instance was the settlement of basic disputes and diminution of mistrusts between Spanish elite factions associated with the Franco regime and those subjugated by the regime but resurgent after Franco's death in 1975 (Gunther 1992; Linz and Stepan 1996, 87–115). King Juan Carlos appointed a former *Franquist* minster, Adolpho Suarez, as prime minister, and in that role, Suarez displayed much political courage and dexterity between 1976 and 1978. He persuaded the Franquist-dominated parliament to dissolve itself, superintended the election of a constituent assembly, released hundreds of political prisoners, legalized the Communist Party after persuading its leaders to abandon their opposition to a constitutional monarchy, and effected reconciliations with dissident regional elites. Importantly, Suarez engineered a set of elite pacts, the Moncloa Pacts, designed to reform Franquist political institutions, secularize the education system, and limit strike activity by trade unions affiliated with the Communist and Socialist Parties. Since the remarkable elite accommodations orchestrated by Suarez, competitions between factions have been restrained, even amid the severe economic crisis that gripped Spain after 2009 and ravages of the COVID-19 virus during 2020–2021.

Consensual unified elites have also originated in the *attainment of independence* by former colonies, in which local native-born elites practiced a restrained home rule politics while waging long and sometimes violent struggles for independence. As happened in each of Britain's North American colonies, local elites in partially self-governing colonies may develop a high enough level of mutual trust when resisting the colonial power's intrusions that the national elites they form after independence are consensually unified. In addition to the United States and Canada, this was the experience of local elites in New Zealand and Australia during the latter part of the nineteenth century and of similar elites in Ireland, South Africa, and India during the twentieth century's first half. (Strictly speaking, it was several separate colonial entities that attained independence with elites that were consensually unified and subsequently merged to form national consensually unified elites in the United States, Australia, and South Africa.)

It is worth noting that elites in the most prominent United Dutch Provinces, especially Holland, achieved consensual unity before and during their successful struggle for independence from Spain late in the sixteenth century, although full national integration of Dutch elites and provinces did not occur until after the Napoleonic Wars. Elites in Switzerland also became consensually unified from the time of the country's consolidation in 1848. Consensual unity appears to have been the elite configuration in most, if not all, of the previously independent Swiss cantons and probably dated back to their earlier independence struggles.

Where consensually unified elites formed during independence struggles, local elites had earlier played significant roles in representative institutions allowed by colonial governments. The roles afforded a considerable practice of limited and restrained politics (Weiner 1987). This was not the case, however, in Latin American colonies controlled by Spain and Portugal, where, moreover, there was little clear understanding of territorial boundaries when independence was attained. Consequently, military leaders tended to predominate at independence and for long periods thereafter. Nor were the political experiences of elites under colonial rule and when struggling for independence propitious for consensual unity in more than a few of the scores of countries that became independent states during the decades after World War II. Except in India, Malaya (later Malaysia), Senegal, and a handful of small former British colonies, such as Jamaica and Barbados, independence brought elite disunity and political instability.

To summarize, there were two ways in which consensually unified elites formed historically: (1) through sudden and basic settlements in societies at a relatively low level of socioeconomic development and (2) through colonial home rule and an independence struggle where local elites had already received, or received during their struggle, experience in political bargaining and restrained competition. Neither of these historical origins appears relevant to countries in which elites are disunified in today's world, although the settlement in Spain, parts of which had reached an industrial level of development by the 1970s, has been a conspicuous exception. In general, factions in disunified elites today are probably too numerous and too closely tied to non-elite interests to be able to fashion settlements. As for consensually unified elites emerging through home rule tutelage and an independence struggle, colonial rule is a condition that no longer seriously exists. These observations raise the question of whether there may be a third way in which consensual unified elites might form. To address this, I want to consider what might be termed imperfectly unified elites.

IMPERFECTLY UNIFIED ELITES

Imperfectly unified elites differ from consensually unified elites in that unity and mutual trust exist mainly among conservative political forces and do not extend to a large, conspicuous, and separate elite faction or set of factions that have usually been of socialist persuasion. A precarious stability of political institutions emanates from the demonstrated ability of the relatively unified portion of elites to maintain control by winning electoral majorities repeatedly. Consequently, veto groups centered on military commanders in countries where elites have previously been disunified cease to function as such, and expectations of military interventions in politics recede. Riots and disorders remain common, but irregular seizures of executive power seem increasingly unlikely. Discontented leftist (or possibly extreme rightist) elites show their frustration by fomenting popular disorders but are dissuaded by considerations of expediency and perhaps democratic principle from making frontal assaults on institutions that seem to command repeated majority support in elections.

While political settlements in disunified elites usually occur at a low level of socioeconomic development, stability created by imperfectly unified elites seems to occur only at a relatively high level.

This is because it is only at a fairly high level of development that it is occasionally possible to demonstrate, through repeated electoral victories, the existence of reliably moderate majorities in electorates. Only when such a development level is reached do majorities of voters come to have a stake in the political status quo or some close approximation of it (see table 1.1).

The clearest example is Japan after the end of U.S. occupation following World War II and once Japan's spectacular economic recovery was well advanced. Conservative elite factions, consolidating in the Liberal Democratic Party (LDP) late in the 1950s, began to command reliable electoral majorities and, hence, control of parliamentary and executive authority. A large but minority portion of Japanese voters regularly supported several left-wing parties that bitterly opposed the dominant LDP. Riots and sometimes violent protests against government policies were mounted by opposition party elites, but there was never any real prospect they would topple established institutions.

Belgium, probably for the whole period from its national independence in 1830 until the 1960s, also illustrated the precarious stability achieved through imperfect elite unity. Although subject to frequent left versus right clashes in the streets and growing divisions between Flemish and Walloon regions, there was always majority support for conservative and moderate forces in parliament, and the stability of Belgian political institutions was not in basic doubt. The stability of Norwegian and Danish institutions from the date of Norway's de facto independence from Sweden in 1884 and Denmark's embrace of cabinet responsibility to parliament in 1901 can be explained similarly. Deep divisions between conservative and radical socialist elite factions were apparent in both Scandinavian countries down to the 1930s, but there were steady electoral majorities for conservative and centrist parties, and institutional stability never seemed in doubt.

The possibility that imperfectly unified elites may evolve into consensual unified elites is likely, although not certain. During the 1970s one country in which to watch for such an evolution was France. Repeated conservative Gaullist electoral and referendum victories after 1958 suggested that French elites were imperfectly unified rather than disunified, as they had clearly been throughout

French history down to General de Gaulle's political ascendance in
a situation of near civil war brought about by the Algerian crisis in
1958. During the 1970s consolidation of French leftist elites, including most of the Communist Party elite, into elites merely contesting
for institutionalized power with the Gaullists and their centrist allies
began to approximate the moderate competitions that unfold in
countries where elites are consensual unified. Since the Mitterrand
Socialist government's abandonment of radical economic policies
in the early 1980s, it has been apparent that French elites are unified, and the political system is for the first time in French history
reliably stable.

QUESTIONS OF PROOF

Elites become ideological or consensual unified in specific circumstances that might be expected to have one or the other effect. As
foregoing cases illustrate, such circumstances can be quite closely
dated, and after their occurrence irregular seizures of power such as
military coups or uprisings that military forces refrain from repressing are not observed and not regarded by political actors as serious
possibilities. Similarly, elites of either kind become disunified, if at
all, only in circumstances identifiable as likely to have that effect.
Where circumstances plausibly suggest that previously unified elites
have become disunified, occasional or frequent seizures of power
will be observed or thought to be serious possibilities by political
actors.

   In terms of method, the *observable absence* of seizures of
power in polities after appropriate and specifiable circumstances
that occurred in the past warrants a *presumption* of elite unity (for
instance, British elites after 1689, American elites after 1789, Swedish elites after 1809, Soviet elites after 1922, Spanish elites after
1978). Conversely, the equally *observable occurrence* or widely
expected occurrence of simple seizures of power in polities whose
histories display *no circumstances* in which the creation of elite
unity could reasonably be thought to have taken place warrants the
presumption that elites are disunified.

The focus is on elite unity because modern history shows that, once attained, it strongly tends to be *reliably self-perpetuating*. Of course, massive intervention by an external force, as in full military conquest or coercion through the threat of organized warfare, can destroy any feature of a society, not least the character of its elites. It makes no difference whether such destruction is civil or international in source. Nor can elite unity be counted on to prevent the organization of a rival regime on some corner of a national territory. If organized warfare results, the rival regime might conceivably conquer the territory over which unified elites have presided. However, this would not be the "simple seizure of power" that elite unity precludes.

Another exception to the contention that elite unity is reliably self-perpetuating must be noted. If a society is deeply divided along clear *geographic lines* into linguistic, cultural, religious, economic, or some combination of such divisions, this will not necessarily prevent elites from becoming or remaining unified. But such geographically demarcated divisions may operate eventually to break up elite unity along lines like those dividing the general population. A country in which elites are unified might be subjected to regional secession, perhaps followed by civil war, although in such a case, elites in one or both parts of the former national territory might continue to be unified. This was probably true, for example, of consensual unified elites in the Confederacy and the Union during the American Civil War.

Even without secession or civil war, subnational *geographically demarcated* differences in culture or interests might break up elite unity. Elites in Yugoslavia were a case in point. They were ideological unified after a tiny band of Communist (Partisan) leaders took power at the end of World War II and erected a Socialist Federal Republic that consisted of six geographically, ethnically, economically, and, in some instances, religiously and linguistically distinct republics. During the 1960s the several republics' discordant identities and economic interests eroded the ideological unity of national elites because representatives of the republics increasingly pursued the diverging interests of their culturally, linguistically, and otherwise distinct republics. By 1972, national elites had become segmented along republic lines (Klansjek and Flere 2019). After Josip Broz Tito died in 1980, elite segmentation accelerated, and in June 1991 elites in the two wealthiest republics, Slovenia and Croatia, declared independence. This unleashed a hecatomb of "ethnic cleansing," and for all practical purposes the Federal Republic of Yugoslavia ceased to exist a year later.

Elites in the Soviet Union were another case in point. During the 1970s and 1980s, growing economic difficulties eroded the credibility of the single communist ideology elite members were required to express. After 1985, Mikhail Gorbachev's *perestroika* and *glasnost* doctrines showed there was little ideological elite unity left, and a failed coup attempt in August 1991 indicated clear elite disunity. At the end of 1991, geographically demarcated cultural and economic divisions led the Union's constituent republics to declare independence and the Union ceased to exist in the last days of 1991.

Thus, two sets of circumstances might terminate ideological or consensual elite unity: (1) destruction or grave weakening by organized warfare, whether civil or international, or (2) deep divisions of cultural or economic interests along subnational geographic lines. In the language of formal theorizing, both sets of circumstances are outside this chapter's *universe of discourse*. In other words, the flat contention is that polities in which elites are unified, whether in ideological or consensual form, will not experience simple seizures of power and will sustain political stability indefinitely when circumstances outside the universe of discourse are not present. Once established, elite unity is reliably self-perpetuating no matter what the behavior of non-elites or other forces within the specified universe of discourse may be.

Does this mean that generalizations in this chapter cannot address societies with characteristics that lie outside the universe of discourse? No. Predictions about political stability or instability in such societies can be made. But if they turn out to be erroneous because of circumstances specifically excluded from the universe of discourse, the generalizations from which such predictions stem are not thereby invalidated.

NON-ELITES AND POLITICS

Marx held that the orientations people hold toward politics are shaped most basically by relationships of economic production in which they find themselves. A person's view of political power and its exercise arises primarily out of his or her experience of power in the workplace and work-related contexts. Contrary to Marx's expectation, however, when societies successfully undergo socioeconomic development, relationships of economic production evolve in such a way that the orientations people hold toward politics change from predominantly egalitarian in preindustrial conditions to predominantly nonegalitarian in postindustrial conditions. In between, during the industrial stage of development, non-elites are deeply divided between those with egalitarian and those with anti-egalitarian orientations. This reversal of Marx's expectation stems from the changing sizes of three basic components of any workforce during socioeconomic development—agricultural and artisan, manual industrial, nonmanual bureaucratic and service—and thus on the changing prevalence of the political orientation characteristic of each component.

Agricultural and artisan workers are distinguished by their need to pay constant attention to the *material environment*. Plowing a field, caring for animals, hunting, driving a truck, fixing a machine, and fabricating objects for sale requires the worker to assess his or her material surroundings and decide alone or in concert with familial or other close associates how to organize immediate work tasks. Whether agricultural and artisan work is totally free of more general supervision, whether the worker is a subordinate in wider economic or social relations, or whether he or she is exploited or left alone is largely irrelevant to the decisions that immediate work tasks require. In short, agricultural and artisan work does not lend itself to thorough and close supervision; when performing it, the typical worker has substantial autonomy.

By contrast, persons belonging to the manual industrial or to the nonmanual bureaucratic and service component of a workforce must pay close attention to the *social environment*. To be useful, their work must mesh in reasonably efficient and harmonious ways with the work of many others in the context of specific organizational arrangements. The worker must react to and often forecast accurately the decisions of persons and groups who are usually socially or physically remote from her or him. Manual work in large manufacturing, mining, and construction enterprises is determined by supervisors' instructions. There the worker needs to apply and, indeed, is allowed to apply only a minimal degree of thought to tasks that involve relationships that are normally semi-hostile with bosses and supervisors. The manual industrial worker's interests lie primarily in limiting the time and energy devoted to work while getting as much compensation for it as possible. These interests impel the worker to appraise and calculate his or her personal relations with bosses and supervisors and with workmates who have similar interests.

The nonmanual bureaucratic and service component of a workforce includes the most important and influential persons in a society—insofar as they are not members of a leisure class, as many such persons were historically. But the bureaucratic and service component is by no means limited to executives, managers, officials, and persons in the professions; it includes large numbers of record-keeping personnel, communications and sales personnel, providers of many kinds of personal services, and, in general, all those whose work involves dealing with members of the public in some meaningful economic context. Bureaucratic and service work requires that close attention be paid to its social setting, either because the work involves influencing or attempting to influence the behavior of others (as with lawyers, teachers, therapists, and members of other professions) or because it is meshed complexly with the work of other persons and organizations, near and far, and must be coordinated deliberately with them. Unlike manual industrial workers, the thought and planning in which bureaucratic and service workers engage are integral parts of the work process itself and not mainly or merely efforts to protect their personal interests against those of bosses, supervisors, and enterprises employing them. Unlike manual industrial work, moreover, bureaucratic and service work occasionally or frequently brings those who perform it into contact with influential and powerful persons.

Table 1.1.   Modal sizes of workforce components during modern history

Workforce component	Preindustrial	Industrial	Postindustrial
Agriculture and artisan	about 80%	70->50%	35->5%
Manual industrial	4 to 6%	10% or more	35->15%
Bureaucratic and service	10 to 15%	less than 30%	40 to 80%

Source: Adapted from Field and Higley 1980, 25. Transitional sizes of components between stages are not specified. Formulae for calculating these estimates and applications to data for historical occupational change are presented in Field 1967, 37–78.

Based on data covering the evolution of workforces in a score of Western countries, plus Japan, during the modern historical period, it is possible to estimate *modal sizes* of the three basic workforce components during the main stages of economic development (see table 1.1).

A broad yet distinctive orientation toward power and politics is characteristic of each workforce component. Ideologies, devised mainly by elites, build on these orientations, making them more conscious, rationalizing and generally molding them into respectable intellectual positions. But underneath complex ideological superstructures, the orientations relate most basically to power and how it is exercised and perceived in work contexts. They relate, that is, to the ability of persons to modify the motivations and conduct of other persons through offers and threats. Inasmuch as this is what politics are all about, the orientations derived from how power is experienced and perceived in processes of work are "political" in the deepest sense. The political actions (or inactions) of non-elites are shaped by their diverse experiences of, and feelings about, *power*.

For agricultural and artisan workers, power is something special; its exercise is not an everyday, routine matter. Power may impinge on how the worker disposes of the crops or artifacts that he or she has grown or fabricated. But from the worker's point of view, power does not impinge in any sensible or rational way on how to raise crops or fabricate artifacts. Most of the time, the agricultural or artisan worker can do without supervision or complex organization; he or she does not need to be told what to do nor need to guess what others will do. When power impinges on the worker's daily tasks ("You must use my grindstone and pay to do so"), it is seen as interference and is not readily accepted. If power is exerted to restrict others from harming the worker's interests, it may be regarded as legitimate. If, for example, incursions of bandits or pirates are likely, the agricultural or artisan worker may willingly support the household of a militarily effective family that fends them off. But the worker is not inclined to support such a household for no good reason.

Not using or needing power to perform work, the agricultural or artisan worker basically regards power as exceptional and peripheral and is not inclined to analyze the logic of events leading to power exercises. Instead power is seen as being used to maintain or extend the *statuses* of the powerful and, perhaps in fortunate circumstances, to protect the worker from depredations by other powerful persons exerting their statuses. Over time, the worker evaluates the legitimacy of powerful persons' statuses in terms of what their occasional exertions of power are likely to do for or against the worker's own interests. He or she does not readily understand the behavior of powerful persons, does not normally empathize with them, and tends to resent their exertions of power unless they afford protection from other power wielders.

When Western societies passed through the preindustrial stage of development, agricultural and artisan workers consistently resented the exactions that well-off and powerful persons made on their resources. When politically activated, those workers tended to think of themselves as the "common people" opposing exploiters. This tendency was counteracted where, as in nineteenth-century France and Spain, agricultural and artisan workers regarded the upper echelons of society as allies against hostile cultural forces, such as anticlericals who threatened to deprive them of valued religious institutions.

When Western countries and Japan passed through the industrial stage, however, agricultural and artisan workers were fewer in number and many were descendants of relatively prosperous agricultural and artisanal families. They were often owners of small properties or aspired to independent ownership of land or artisan enterprises and the equipment necessary for production. Some even employed persons who were situated in or influenced by the manual industrial component, which agricultural and artisan workers tended to fear. Their orientation toward power became more ambivalent than in preindustrial conditions. On the one hand, agricultural and artisan workers still had little understanding of the rationales of power exertions and continued to resent impingements on their own affairs, but on the other, they approved of power exertions that restrained the numerous and impoverished manual industrial workers whom they feared.

Turning to the manual industrial component, its size was small in the preindustrial stage of development, and it consisted mostly of displaced agricultural and artisan workers who no longer had places reserved for them in self-supporting agricultural or artisanal households. Their "rights" to such places had perhaps been bought out, or powerful persons had perhaps deprived them of such rights. Often they were merely surplus young people who managed to survive for a few years in relatively prosperous rural localities in which there was, however, no strong need for their labor. They left those localities more or less voluntarily and drifted to towns where unskilled manual work was available.

So long as manual industrial workers consisted largely of migrants from rural localities, they retained the views of their rural families, thinking of themselves as part of the common people or "the laboring class." But as their numbers grew, manual industrial workers tended to become more consciously and continuously alienated toward powerful persons than their agricultural and artisanal forebears because their work tasks were less mentally absorbing and their living conditions were often more precarious. They had nothing in the way of property, half-grown crops, a stock of artifacts to sell, or some other "business of their own" to mind. In times of serious political tension or conflict, they took readily to the streets in riot or insurrection.

Although comprising only 4 to 6 percent of a preindustrial workforce, the employment of manual industrial workers in small factories, mines, and construction projects clustered them in parts of bourgeoning towns and cities. This forced powerful persons to

give more continuous thought to policing manual industrial workers than had to be given to policing agricultural and artisan workers. Although it seldom happened (France late in the eighteenth
century being the major exception), if manual industrial workers in
the preindustrial stage of development erupted in serious rebellion,
many agricultural and artisan workers and families were inclined to
support them and join in insurrection. In other words, "the masses"
were potentially unified against the upper classes in preindustrial
societies. The overwhelming majority of the workforce was biased
against the existing social order and could sometimes be activated
to destroy it.

Contrary to Marx's thesis about where proletarian revolutions
would occur, this was no longer the case in the industrial stage of
development because agricultural and artisan workers—still comprising half or more of the total workforce—became conscious
of distinct interests that were hostile to those of manual industrial
workers. The latter were numerous and belonged to families in
which the identities and traditions of manual work were passed from
one generation to the next. A "working-class culture" formed and
replaced the attenuated and functionless rural culture that surplus
agricultural and artisan workers had earlier brought into the small
manual industrial component in preindustrial conditions (Thompson
1963).

Manual industrial workers were watchers of people and society
rather than of crops and materials. Their interests lay in relation to
other people, and in relatively free Western societies they formed
their own institutions: trade unions, consumer cooperatives, and
political parties. Except in very prosperous or geographically mobile
industrial societies, such as the United States and Canada during
the late nineteenth and early twentieth centuries, the orientation of
most manual industrial workers toward the social order was hostile
and radically egalitarian. They felt they had to combat the pressures
and stratagems of those who were better off, and where doctrines
such as socialism were propagated widely, they looked forward to a
time when there would be no better-off people. The irony was that
this kind of mature working-class consciousness, expressed through
distinct and relatively powerful organizations, occurred only at that

point in development—the industrial stage—when much of the workforce was no longer attracted to the prospect of social leveling. The novelty of this irony created much political confusion and violence in Europe during the twentieth century's first half, most notably antisocialist fascist movements and regimes.

During passage through the preindustrial and industrial stages of development, Western societies were undergirded by permanent, increasingly large, and complex bureaucratic organizations necessary for obtaining and sustaining varying degrees of social order. The organizations involved paying wages and salaries to all persons working in them. Governments maintained permanent, paid military and police forces constructed initially to ward off foreign threats but that quickly became prudent checks against domestic disorder. If only to keep up with the expenses incurred thereby, government finance came to require large bodies of tax collectors, record-keepers, appraisers, and even informers.

Beyond such governmental concerns, trading with distant countries and constructing buildings, roads, railways, and other forms of public works quickly exceeded the capacities of strictly family enterprises. These activities required bureaucratic organization, and this demanded, in addition to manual industrial workers employed on a wage-earning basis in factories, mines, and construction sites, many kinds of record-keeping and sales personnel, managers, experts, and professionals. As these categories of nonmanual workers were employed increasingly on a full-time basis, the bureaucratic and service component of Western workforces expanded steadily.

Unlike the power possessed by armed and leisured classes in medieval societies, power in bureaucratic organizations could not be exercised occasionally and capriciously; it was effective only when continuously and shrewdly exerted. Once there were important bureaucracies, in other words, being seriously influential became something like a full-time job. This was because too much was at stake, and others would grab the plum if the holder of a strategic bureaucratic position was careless or lazy in important matters. Strategic power in bureaucratic organizations did not always rest in formally constituted positions, of course. The persons who had such power did not always draw their major incomes from the bureaucracies they commanded, nor did they act like regular job holders as regards the hours and locations of their work.

Yet there were always strong tendencies to regularize bureaucratic power positions, and as societies moved from the preindustrial to the industrial stage of development, positions of power increasingly became formal posts on organizational charts, carrying substantial salaries. In this way, powerful individuals comprising elites became members of the bureaucratic and service component themselves. Like middle-level managers and many other categories of nonmanual personnel, they became bureaucrats and service providers devoting something like their full time and energy to managing and regulating an extended and impersonal (that is, nonfamilial) organization.

Two effects flowed from the bureaucratization of power. First, in a way that agricultural workers and artisans never do, nonmanual workers came to understand power in complex organizations as a tool for getting work done. Second, unlike the work situations of agricultural, artisan, and manual industrial workers, the work situations of nonmanual personnel did not contain any general barrier that prevented empathy with the motives, dilemmas, and predicaments of the influential and powerful. Rather, nonmanual workers came to see power, in the sense of manipulating the motivation and behavior of other persons through threats and offers, as routinely necessary to getting organizational and service work done. They were, consequently, not inclined to judge power in terms of the legitimacy of a power wielder's social status. They tended to judge a power act's legitimacy based on whether it served a proper organizational purpose or function. If they thought it did, then the question of whether the power wielder acted within his or her defined sphere of authority (or status) was relatively unimportant. If they thought it did not, they were inclined to condemn the power wielder even if there was no question that he or she acted in accordance with organizationally prescribed authority.

Generalizations about the political orientation of bureaucratic and service workers are more difficult to make than those about orientations of agricultural-artisan and manual industrial workers. This is because the individual situations of nonmanual bureaucratic and service workers differ greatly, ranging from those of elite persons to those of the most harassed and poorly compensated clerks, salespersons, hairdressers, and waitpersons. Yet there is always a tendency among such workers to identify with power wielders; if not with current ones, then with those who might replace them. This is because nonmanual workers not only associate with influential persons or, at least, with others who associate with them, but in important ways they live and behave as the influential do. Their work does not get them dirty, and they may (or must) dress like an influential person.

Like the influential, moreover, the nonmanual worker "works" over luncheons, at receptions, during what is ostensibly recreation, and in other essentially leisured settings. She or he is evaluated at least partly in social terms, that is, whether bosses and colleagues like and trust her or him. All this implies that, while they may not always approve of society's current leaders, bureaucratic and service workers are basically allegiant to the social order, at least in the abstract. They are to important degrees contrivers and maintainers of it and will not readily collaborate in its destruction.

Summarizing to this point, in preindustrial societies there was little significant bureaucratic organization associated with dominant persons who had, however, to work steadily at gaining and retaining their dominance. Although they could count on some empathy from the small number of bureaucratic and service workers, dominant persons presided over social orders in which the great majority of workers (the large agricultural and artisan and the small manual industrial components combined) were potentially alienated by their work situations and could sometimes be activated in leveling movements.

In industrial societies, bureaucratic organization was much more prevalent, and the bureaucratic and service component was of substantial size. The manual industrial component was also large, self-conscious, and alienated from the existing social order. However, it was the only workforce component of which this could be said during the industrial stage of development. Neither the equally large bureaucratic and service component nor the remaining but diminishing agricultural and artisan component was consistently alienated from the industrial social order. Instead both components reacted with hostility to serious leveling initiatives emanating from the alienated manual industrial component. This tended, *pace* Marx, to prevent any sharply egalitarian movements from becoming ascendant during passage through the industrial stage.

ELITES AND NON-ELITES IN POSTINDUSTRIAL POLITICS

In socioeconomic development's postindustrial stage, bureaucratic and service workers are so numerous that they are present in most nuclear families. This presence plus the workers' educations, communication skills, and occupational prestige ensure that their managerial orientation toward power spreads widely through society, muffling what remains of political orientations among greatly reduced numbers of agricultural-artisan and manual-industrial workers. By the early 1970s, all the societies that had reached development's postindustrial stage had done so with elites that were consensual unified (the Anglo-American and Scandinavian societies, the Netherlands, Switzerland), and in several societies that were reaching this stage elites were imperfectly unified (Austria, Belgium, France, Italy, Japan, West Germany). By the 1970s also, a few societies in which elites were ideological unified (Hungary, Czechoslovakia, East Germany, the Soviet Union) displayed workforce configurations close to postindustrial.

The question is how elites and non-elites affect each other in postindustrial conditions. In the countries that first attained postindustrial configurations, the political stability associated with consensual unified elites appeared to deepen. The preponderance of bureaucratic and service workers blurred class lines and weakened customary partisan alignments among non-elites. Elites needed to have less recourse to ideologies such as liberalism and socialism to justify their statuses, policy positions, and governing actions. Their political discourse shifted to discussing affluence and the welfare state as solvents of historical conflicts. Intellectuals avidly discussed the "end of ideology," a thesis that is probably best regarded in hindsight as rationalizing blandly optimistic views of the postindustrial political landscape as viewed from the vantage point of elites.

With high productivity and nearly full employment, the absence of serious economic downturns, a shrunken working class rapidly approaching middle-class lifestyles, and no other large and obviously discontented collectivities in sight (apart from racial minorities suffering systematic discrimination in some countries), there was the appearance of considerable non-elite harmony. Consequently, elites adopted a more blatantly managerial posture and voiced the complacent belief that mere "fair" treatment of individuals and groups would ensure an indefinite continuation of social progress and political tranquility (Field and Higley 1980, 1–17).

Are there grounds for thinking that consensual unified elites are reliably self-perpetuating in postindustrial conditions? There are some reasons to doubt it. Over time, the greater non-elite harmony and elite complacency that were initial effects of postindustrialism diminish. Deteriorating social conditions become apparent in cities, a seemingly intractable form of poverty spreads in urban slums and rural backwaters, and many young people with affluent family backgrounds begin to display much alienation and discontent. Polarizing trends in elites become noticeable, most conspicuously in the United States and United Kingdom, the two countries that have been longest in postindustrial conditions. These trends suggest that politics in advanced postindustrial conditions are difficult to manage.

The postindustrial workforce is in important respects the terminus of socioeconomic development. It completes the conversion of workforces that consisted overwhelmingly of agricultural and artisan workers at development's outset into workforces suffused with bureaucratic and service personnel. It is unlikely that a further stage of development, involving new basic types of work, new workforce components, and new non-elite political orientations, lies beyond the postindustrial stage. If the postindustrial workforce is the end point in development, it must be asked whether societies that have reached it can remain viable politically without the sense of progress and spread of hope that development engendered historically. Put bluntly, can advanced postindustrial societies "stagnate" indefinitely without, to borrow the title of a book by George Packer, "unwinding" socially and politically (2013)?

Perhaps consensual unified elites can in some fashion find ways to make an essentially stagnating, rather than evolving, workforce configuration acceptable to non-elites. There are obstacles, however. One is the increased personal ties between elites and non-elites. In postindustrial societies, persons ascend to elite status from non-elite origins much more frequently than in the rigidly stratified societies of earlier socioeconomic stages. Consequently, elites tend to see themselves as indistinct from non-elites, among whom they have intimate personal associates and for whom they have considerable empathy.

Personal ties between elites and non-elites help to ensure that elites are better able to determine measures that at least partially assuage non-elite discontents and aspirations. But what might happen when and if it is not possible to do this? Presumably, elite actions and measures ranging from discouragement to deception to outright repression would be much harder for non-elites to accept. Disseminations of "conspiracy theories" about elites through social media and eschatological beliefs among spreading millenarian cults are portents at present. One can only suppose that elites will handle such heightened anti-elite animosities once their nature and causes are more clearly understood. Elites may become more collectively conscious of their distinctive responsibilities.

It is not possible to be as sanguine about a still wider difficulty in postindustrial conditions. In all earlier development stages, political action was not generally required to keep most persons steadily engaged in the performance of necessary work. For the most part, internalized attitudes and customary social controls supplied by neighbors and work associates sufficed. In advanced postindustrial conditions, however, social controls, along with religious and other traditional belief systems, attenuate. Non-elite persons increasingly "bowl alone" (Putnam 2000). In earlier stages as well, most persons worked diligently to stave off dreadful circumstances—dismissal, eviction, hunger—and a significant proportion worked without surcease because they could plausibly believe that by doing so their personal ambitions would be realized. Only a small number of specially favored persons—mainly the offspring or friends of the rich and powerful—were unmotivated to work in disciplined ways and were inclined toward a self-indulgent, if perhaps esthetically satisfying, leisure.

It is easy to see that the proportion of people who are unmotivated for steady work, or for whose labor there is no longer a clear and pressing need, increases markedly in materially affluent, technologically advanced, and empathetically indulgent postindustrial conditions. It is useless to ignore this by holding that modern technology greatly reduces the need for human labor. Responsible work is not readily parceled out in little pieces in any society. Some tasks must still—and presumably must always—be performed with care, diligence, and forethought, and those who perform them will not allow a large body of idle people, however decorative they may be, to receive substantial rewards for their idleness. This disjunction between the diligent and the idle signals a growing non-elite divide between "insiders" and "outsiders," although it remains uncertain if it will be of a magnitude that elites are unable to manage (Higley 2016, 144–48).

ELITE AND NON-ELITE LIMITS ON POLITICS

When generalizing about politics, predictive aspirations must be modest because elites are often able to effect important political changes independent of non-elites. Whether elites will do so cannot be inferred from readily quantifiable features of non-elites. For example, neither the creation nor persistence of ideological or consensual unified elites is discernibly linked with non-elite configurations. The probability of a unified elite of either kind forming and of then creating stable political institutions can only be guessed at from a knowledge of a particular elite's recent history. Does it record costly but essentially inconclusive warfare between opposing factions who, in consequence, may be disposed toward a sudden and basic settlement of their disputes? Have elites suffered a defeat so grave that the way may be open for a well-organized but previously peripheral group to seize and consolidate power? Generalizations must allow leeway for such possibilities and elite changes they may entail.

But are generalizations useful when so much latitude must be given to historical accident and contingent circumstance? The generalizations in this chapter are plausible *only* if this limitation is accepted. They are concerned not with what *will* happen, or even what is *likely* to happen—both basically unknowable—but with what will *not* happen or is quite *unlikely* to happen. In the sphere of politics this is not negligible knowledge, and it is probably as much as can be hoped for. Ensuing chapters, especially 2, 3, and 5, assemble this knowledge.

Non-elites, conceived in terms of distinct workforce configurations and associated experiences of, and orientations toward, power, are parameters within which elites act. Specific workforce configurations *prevent* specific kinds of actions by elites in different socioeconomic stages, but they do not determine what elites will do in each stage. In the preindustrial stage, non-elites consist primarily of agricultural and artisan workers plus a small number of laborers making up an incipient manual industrial component. All these workers tend toward a hostile view of power exercises by those who comprise elites, and their impoverished situations give them little reason to fear a general leveling of the existing status order. This forces elites to couch appeals for non-elite support in terms of religious and other traditional beliefs or in terms of some more or less egalitarian ideology. If elites are exceptionally incompetent or unlucky, a collapse of government authority that triggers a leveling revolution is possible, although the reconstruction of elite dominance in some form can be counted on after a short interval.

In the industrial stage, by contrast, the proportions of agricultural and artisan, manual industrial, and bureaucratic and service workers are more nearly equal in size. Although farmers and artisans retain their customary, hostile view of elite power exercises, the fact that significant numbers of them enjoy modest affluence and own small properties and enterprises means that, as a social category, agricultural and artisan workers are no longer receptive to, and may in fact oppose, leveling sentiments voiced by large numbers of alienated manual industrial workers and political parties purporting to represent them. If mobilized by antileveling elite factions, many farmers and artisans will join with bureaucratic and service workers, who feel even more threatened by leveling sentiments, to support authoritarian or even fascist seizures or takeovers of government power aimed at preserving and extending the existing status order by crushing leveling movements. While a shift to authoritarian or fascist rule is possible in the industrial stage, what is *not* possible, that is, what is precluded by the non-elite makeup, is a successful leveling revolution. Contrary to Marx's prediction, no such revolution has ever occurred in an industrial society.

Except in the rarest of circumstances (for example, in the more modernized parts of Spain two or three years after Franco's death in 1975), the non-elite makeup in an industrial society also precludes sudden and deliberate settlements of basic disputes between factions in disunified elites. The relative complexity of industrial society makes elites large and no longer isolated socially from non-elites. Many elite actors give their first allegiance to the partisan interests of the organizations and movements they lead. Negotiating behind the political stage to compromise principled interest positions that factions in elites have repeatedly taken when mobilizing non-elite support and then getting all or most elite members to endorse such compromises is most unlikely. More likely is an imperfectly unified elite whose conservative and moderate factions mobilize a reliable majority of voters disposed to defend the existing status order or a close approximation of it. This depends, however, on choices that elites may or may not make.

Once established, a unified elite of either the consensual or ideological kind is reliably self-perpetuating, regardless of non-elite configurations. In other words, unified elites prevail over non-elites. Through basic elite settlements or propitious colonial political experiences and independence struggles, consensual unified elites formed in a handful of preindustrial societies and persisted without interruption during passage through all subsequent stages of development. Despite deep non-elite cleavages, consensual unified elites of more recent vintage appear to exist in India, Malaysia, Senegal, and Mexico and have persisted to the present.

Ideological unified elites in the Soviet Union lasted for seventy years, and Yugoslav elites lasted for about three decades, until neither was any longer able to contain geographically concentrated cultural and economic divisions that lie outside this chapter's universe of discourse. Not confronting such crippling geographic divisions, ideological unified elites in North Korea, China, and what was North Vietnam have persisted for time periods comparable to the former Soviet elite's duration and give little indication of suffering its fate in the foreseeable future. Whether this will be true of the ideological unified elites in Cuba and Iran, which at present are marking sixty and forty years in power, respectively, are open questions.

CONCLUDING OBSERVATIONS

The generalizations in this chapter will be distasteful to many because they rule out the more ideal aims and outcomes that are regularly voiced by intellectuals and mass media and loosely anticipated by social scientists. They leave no place for idealized visions of democracy or revolution nor a place for the spread of new values that dispose human beings toward a consistent altruism. Human conflicts inevitably dilute social cohesion and constitute political problems that elites must manage as best they can. If, in the end, politics are efforts to maintain some practical degree of social peace by shrewdly and continuously managing the conflicts that regularly arise in societies, politics can never be so effective as to abolish politics.

What is the use of participating in politics that can never be abolished? This question can only be answered in terms of an individual's circumstances. The individual who is an effective member of elites has no choice to make because her or his life is immersed in politics. An elite member does have some effect on incipient or open conflicts in society by reallocating valued things among conflicting groups while encouraging or blocking the pressures of various groups for concessions. The elite person seldom questions seriously whether political action is worthwhile because she or he is aware that some things are different in the world, at least in details, because of the choices the elite person and her or his colleagues have made.

Entering political activities is more problematic for a non-elite person. Such an individual can only slightly reshape the problems with which elites must deal. The chances of advancing to an elite position are small. Why, then, act politically? Often the question answers itself. The non-elite person who has a reasonably satisfactory occupational and personal status is unlikely to give much thought to real political involvement. The non-elite person whose status is in some way threatened by current trends or who is hopelessly restricted by the inadequate circumstances of the social category to which she or he belongs looks for a political opportunity. If it is available, this person may become involved in politics because it is the only way to ward off threats or improve her or his lot.

If one is not driven into politics or does not find political activities personally satisfying, it is pointless to enter politics out of a sense of duty. It is pointless because attention to political matters cannot be rationed, as one might ration contributions to a charity or a church, merely giving political activity what attention "good citizenship" seems to require. Those who participate in politics to satisfy deep needs and pressures, or even those who just play in politics for the fun of it, always invest the extra efforts and time necessary to succeed in their political projects. The dutiful but occasional participant will be outmaneuvered by the more driven or fun-seeking player.

Nevertheless, political participation often provides satisfaction for non-elite persons who like to regard themselves as contributing to a well-ordered and humane society. At least some detailed aspects of their society's functioning are affected by their judgments and skills. But this assumes the existence of consensual unified or at least imperfectly unified elites whose members have managed to create and maintain stable political institutions. In all other circumstances, politics are a compulsive and dangerous activity. Penalties for being associated with a losing side not infrequently extend to losing one's life or liberty. Nor is there any way, seen through the prism of this chapter, for ordinary citizens to transform this dire but historically quite normal situation into a safer and more peaceful one.

Implications of the generalizations presented here are not entirely bleak. They are compatible with a view that people, whether elite or non-elite, can act consequentially according to what politics currently permit. Although we can be reasonably certain that some things that we imagine and that at least some of us wish for will not happen, the limits of politics and what political action can accomplish are still relatively wide.

Chapter Two

Elites, Non-Elites, and Revolution

There is no agreed on definition of "revolution" that attaches the term to a clearly specified political event or process. It is sometimes taken to mean almost any irregular and forcible seizure of power, thereby covering the many coups and sporadic uprisings that occur where elites are disunified. "Revolution" is also often used to label civil wars and wars of liberation that center on dynastic, ethnic, regional, or religious divisions. This definitional vagueness makes it a matter of subjective judgment whether to call a regime, movement, or violent conflict "revolutionary." By not distinguishing between many kinds of violent upheavals, "revolution" has lacked the precision required of a concept that can be utilized seriously when generalizing about elites, non-elites, and politics.

There is, however, one special kind of upheaval that has features objectively different from those of coups, civil wars, secessions, and popular uprisings. This is an upheaval that begins when normal governmental authority, most manifest in disciplined military and police forces, suddenly and dramatically collapses (Brinton 1938; Tilly 1978). During the shorter or longer interval that follows, maintaining order against riot or pillage becomes highly problematic until government authority and military and police discipline are either restored or built anew by some victorious group. One cannot say that elites of any of the four kinds distinguished in chapter 1 exist during the interval. Instead power resides, as radicals like to say, "in the people" or, more precisely, in persons who assemble spontaneously, usually under arms, and respond to immediate propaganda and oratory with mass actions. Such assemblages typically include bodies of rank-and-file troops who have either liquidated their officers or are simply ignoring their orders.

An upheaval of this kind eventually brings a substantially different body of persons to elite status, and it changes political and especially economic institutions in fundamental ways. But before such sweeping alterations become apparent, whoever attempts to restore or construct a semblance of organized power in the area where governmental authority has collapsed usually comes under attack from geographic areas to which the collapse has not extended. To survive the attack, the new power organizers must quickly create some degree of bureaucratic centralization accompanied by disciplined military and police units. Sooner or later, the popular assemblages that have held forth are policed and repressed. When this happens, the observer can again speak of a regime operated by elites of one of the four kinds. In the English and French upheavals of 1642–1651 and 1789–1794, respectively, the new elites were again disunified and the regimes they operated were unstable. But after the Russian upheaval (1917–1921) and after the Shah's regime collapsed in Iran during 1977–1978, elites were ideological unified because of the victorious Bolsheviks' and the Shi'ites' tight organization and doctrinal cohesion during the upheavals.

If for purposes of conceptual order and terminological consistency "revolution" refers only to an upheaval involving the collapse of governmental authority and an ensuing interval when coercive power is in spontaneous popular assemblages, it is a rare and unlikely event. A revolution in this sense can probably occur only in societies at low levels of socioeconomic development, that is, largely agrarian or peasant societies. In more bureaucratized societies at higher development levels, the widespread collapse of government authority and disciplined military and police forces seems even more implausible today than it did when proponents of revolution counted, for the most part mistakenly, on large numbers of citizen-soldiers turning on governments after hardships and defeats in large-scale warfare. Indeed, advances in military technology, especially nuclear weapons, suggest that wars fought by mass armies may now be relics of history. These considerations imply only two possibilities for revolution and its consequences. In one, revolution reconfigures but does not transcend a disunified pattern of elite behavior. In the other, revolution effects a sweeping circulation that ushers in a new and hegemonic elite. I propose to examine revolutions that have exemplified each possibility.

REVOLUTION AND ELITE RECONFIGURATION

If analysis is limited to independent national states, less than a handful of the many upheavals that dotted the modern historical record prior to the Russian Revolution of 1917–1921 constituted a leveling "revolution" in the sense of the term here. All were egalitarian in thrust, but all were essentially rejuvenating upheavals: they infused existing elites with new members and altered inequalities between rulers and ruled in some measure but did not create a new and hegemonic elite. This was the case in three watershed revolutions: England 1648–1649, France 1789–1794, and Mexico 1912–1917.

The English, French, and Mexican revolutions each occurred in a preindustrial society in which elites were deeply disunified. Peasants and their families comprised the overwhelming bulk of England's population in 1640 (Moore 1966, 143), more than 80 percent of the French population in the 1780s (Skocpol 1979, 54), and as much as 87 percent of the Mexican population in 1910 (Hart 1987, 258). In each country, elite power struggles had been chronic. A three-way struggle between monarchical, ecclesiastical, and landowning elites in England gradually simplified, after Henry VIII's dissolution of monasteries in 1536, into a face-off between monarchical and landowning ("gentry") elites (Lachmann 1987; 1989). Consolidation of the French state during the sixteenth and seventeenth centuries involved continuous elite violence: protracted civil war between 1562–1598; assassination of two kings, Henry III and Henry IV; and the nobility's armed resistance to the monarchy in the Fronde uprising of 1648–1653. During the eighteenth century, French elites were increasingly split into two opposing camps: one upholding monarchy, the Church, aristocratic privilege, and the general importance of tradition; the other consisting of leaders of the growing professional and bourgeois class, who preached a rationalistic gospel that social and political institutions were legitimate only to the extent they achieved good purposes. In Mexico after independence from Spain in 1810, chaotic struggles between conservative and liberal and between federal and provincial elite groups involved numerous uprisings, assassinations, and regime overthrows that culminated in Porfirio Díaz's 1875–1876 rebellion and the start of his repressive seven terms as president.

A regime crisis involving serious political miscalculations by ruling elites opened the door to revolution in each country. After he dissolved the English parliament in 1629, Charles I and his government ministers underestimated the cost of suppressing a Scottish rebellion, and in 1640 Charles was forced to summon parliament, after holding the first parliamentary elections in twelve years, to raise needed revenues. More interested in airing grievances than rubber-stamping Charles's revenue requests, this "short" parliament proved recalcitrant and was dissolved in an unnecessarily heavy-handed and provocative way (Aylmer 1986, 12–15). New elections produced a "long" parliament that contained many dedicated opponents of the king. The opponents proceeded to impeach one of his ministers, purge some of his parliamentary supporters, confront Charles with demands he refused to concede, and eventually create their own army with which to coerce him.

In France during the 1770s and 1780s, military overreach abroad and reform measures at home produced fiscal deficits so large that Louis XVI was forced to look for a political solution to economic difficulties by convening the Estates General for the first time since 1614. The complicated electoral processes this involved, combined with the spread of liberal ideas through a large part of elites by that point, opened opportunities for radical agitation (Schama 1989).

In Mexico, the lengthy Díaz presidency confronted increasing fiscal difficulties and spreading elite opposition after 1905. By using force and fraud to prevent Francisco Madero's election to the presidency in 1910, the *Porfiriato* provoked Madero's armed rebellion in the north, which, coupled with Emiliano Zapata's simultaneous uprising in the south, sealed the Díaz regime's fate and opened the way to revolution (Knight 1986). The collapse of government occurred rapidly in each country. Wide-ranging civil war broke out in England in 1642 and lasted until 1645 when parliamentary forces, having been merged into a zealous "New Model" army led by Oliver Cromwell, defeated the king's forces decisively. By then, however, the New Model army had become a political force in its own right, with many of its officers and cadres holding "Independent" or "Congregationalist" religious views more extreme than those held by most of the army's sponsors in parliament and probably most of the population at large. The danger of civil war between parliamentary factions, an uprising in London against parliament, a mutiny in the New Model army's ranks, and then a quickly repulsed counterattack by Charles's forces in 1648 indicated the effective collapse of government.

In France after the Bastille was stormed in July 1789, the almost total prevalence of rationalist agitation dissolved the authority of the royal bureaucracy and the officer corps, with power gravitating to activists and orators who dominated newly created municipal bodies. The Estates General was replaced by a National Assembly, a body that had some prestige but totally lacked the bureaucratic and military instruments necessary for ruling. A protracted situation of governmental collapse began. In Mexico, Madero replaced Díaz as president in mid-1911, but his failure to placate elite groups who supported him soon led to further rebellions, notably Zapata's in late 1911 and those of several northern leaders during the following spring. By the summer of 1912, the federal government had only the most tenuous control over much of the country, while economic and other national institutions were on the verge of complete breakdown (Hart 1987, 259). A situation of government collapse existed.

The extent of government collapse differed appreciably during the three revolutionary intervals. It was least extensive in England because the New Model army maintained its discipline and political control throughout the revolution's most radical phase. This began with the "long" parliament's order, in November 1648, for the army to disband. Refusing to obey that order on the ground that to do so would be to accept coercion of their religious beliefs, the army's leaders purged parliament of all but a minority whose religious beliefs coincided with theirs. The resulting "rump" parliament immediately declared a republic, put Charles I on trial and executed him, and abolished the House of Lords. The purge of parliament and ensuing regicide were clearly revolutionary acts, which reflected the near dominance of Levelers and other millenarian sects during the winter and early spring of 1648–1649. However, the millenarians' prominence was short lived because in March 1649 the army leadership ordered the arrest of their principal leaders, and that May Cromwell and his associates quickly suppressed a mutiny by army units sympathetic to the Levelers who, after those defeats, were essentially finished. Because the purging of parliament and execution of the king were deeply repugnant to most elite factions and segments of public opinion, including many of the more zealous Presbyterian clergy and laity, support for the republic melted and a compromise "commonwealth" regime, which was also deeply unpopular, was instituted.

Government collapse was much more extensive during the French revolutionary interval. By 1792, royal and church authorities had been swept aside and all privileges had been abolished, but for most people life was obviously no better than it had been before 1789; indeed, in material respects it was much worse. To the most extreme agitators and popular leaders, the only expedient explanation for this state of affairs was that many persons had been so hopelessly corrupted by the *ancien regime* that they were unable to respond to the opportunities a new revolutionary order, based on abstractions of liberty, equality, and fraternity, supposedly offered. On this reasoning, and at the demand of the Paris mob, the Terror began. Between 1792 and 1794, there appeared to be no detailed governing policy other than guillotining persons whose previous lives rendered them unfit to live in a free and equal society; in St. Just's phrase, "The Republic consists in the extermination of everything that opposes it" (Schama 1989, 787).

A collapse of government authority was also extensive during Mexico's revolutionary interval. Having overthrown Díaz in 1911, Madero was himself overthrown and murdered by forces of a

Porfirian general, Victoriano Huerta, in February 1913. This immediately provoked a "Constitutionalist" rebellion led by Venustiano Carranza, the governor of one of the northern states who acted in concert with other northern leaders, notably Alvaro Obregón in the state of Sonora and Pancho Villa in the state of Chihuahua. In July 1914, the Constitutionalists drove Heurta from office, but in doing so they alienated Villa and his peasant-based Army of the North, which was the largest military force organized during the revolution. Late 1914 was "the high point of the rural lower-class revolutionary tide" (Hart 1987, 305). An attempt to reach a *modus vivendi* among the several revolutionary elite groups and movements in the Convention of Aquascalientes resulted only in further radicalization. Carranza was denied the presidency, Zapatistas and Villistas occupied Mexico City, and Carranza's forces withdrew to Vera Cruz. Although the latter soon counterattacked and defeated Villa's army between April and July 1915, most of Mexico, including its cities, was under no centralized government control. Zapatistas and other peasant bands controlled the countryside, while riotous workers espousing radical egalitarian goals dominated Mexico City and other urban areas. In the face of repeated strikes, most public services ceased, and hunger became widespread. Two general strikes took place in 1916, but Carranza, now president, crushed the second of them by force and broke up the principal working-class organizations. This effectively ended the revolution's most radical phase during which military forces fragmented but, as in England, never fully disintegrated.

The character and content of revolutionary ideologies also shape the outcome of revolution. In none of the three cases under discussion were principal revolutionary groups in possession of an especially coherent and plausible ideology. In England, zealous Puritans held generally to "a coercive, intolerant politics of moral reform . . . which saw public enforcement of piety and social discipline to be a way for the elect to honor its God" (Zaret 1989, 169). But many Puritan leaders were loath to impose this belief on others or liquidate those who held rival beliefs. This was crucially true of Cromwell and his military commanders who were in position to do the latter if they had wanted (see Aylmer 1986, 183–86). Nor did most of those leaders place much stock in the secular egalitarian doctrines of the millenarian sects; they were now, after all, core elites and had no intention of renouncing their privileges (Bendix 1978, 32).

French revolutionary groups were, in contrast, much less reticent about imposing their beliefs on everyone else. But those beliefs lacked programmatic coherence and plausibility; they amounted to the utopian insistence that merely repudiating tradition, traditional authorities, and aristocratic privilege would somehow promptly result in a just and happy society. When, by 1792, this recipe for social and political salvation was seen to be failing, the only recourse was indiscriminate terror. Lacking any seriously instrumental scheme for how society could plausibly be structured, French revolutionary ideology was inimical to the careful actions that might have enabled an extremist group to prevail and consolidate power.

Coming much later in the "Age of Ideology," the doctrines of nineteenth-century liberalism, socialism, and democracy were well known to Mexican revolutionary leaders, although not to their mainly peasant followers. But those cogent ideologies were blanketed by deeply held regional and ethnic identities; strong urban-rural antipathies, especially in religious matters; a simplistic populism that grew out of the long experience of village and regional autonomy; and nationalist sentiments and aspirations that cut across class and other social boundaries. Thus, no coherent and compelling ideology served as a unifying vehicle for any of the contending elite groups in the Mexican revolution.

From an analytical standpoint, each of the three revolutions lacked the combination of features—extensive government collapse coupled with a programmatically cogent ideology—that makes the victory of a revolutionary elite likely. Instead, segments of preexisting disunified elites eventually regained control and resumed their internecine struggles. In England in 1653, Cromwell and other army officers dissolved the "rump" parliament, which had continued to sit after the climactic events of 1648–1649, and they instituted a military dictatorship. But as evidenced by its immediate unraveling once Cromwell died in 1658, the dictatorship hardly signified the victory of a revolutionary elite. Indeed, by the time of Cromwell's death most Puritan political leaders were disillusioned and no longer saw much future in keeping a king off the throne. In short order, therefore, the army was purged of its republican elements and became badly divided. Royalist elite factions regained the initiative, parliament dissolved itself, a new parliament was elected, and Charles II was invited to restore monarchy. The elite division over monarchical versus parliamentary power resumed and involved two increasingly distinct camps, Tories and Whigs. Lasting another thirty years, struggles between the camps culminated in the "Glorious Revolution" of 1688–1689, when key leaders of the camps engineered a sudden and basic settlement of their most principled disputes (discussed in chapter 1).

In France, the so-called Thermidorean Reaction of July 1794 brought the revolutionary interval to an outcome similar to that in England during the late 1650s. Without explanation, the National Convention, which had replaced the National Assembly, suddenly voted to arrest and turn over to the revolutionary tribunal its own principal leader, Robespierre. Organized military companies, recruited in the more prosperous parts of Paris, suppressed protests by Robespierre's supporters, and he was executed. Although no one admitted it, the entire thrust of the revolutionary interval changed with that event. Right-wing elite persons, long silent, were immediately heard in political debate and the Terror largely ceased. Over the next five years, administrative and military bureaucracies were reestablished, power was again centralized in Paris, and France began a series of military conquests that spread some of the revolution's more effective bourgeois innovations through much of Europe. But while leaders of the Thermidorean Reaction and the ensuing Directorate eschewed the suicidal measures of the Terror, they clearly constituted a disunified elite as indicated by several coups between 1794 and Napoleon Bonaparte's seizure of power in 1799. Eventually assuming the title of emperor, Bonaparte largely suppressed political debate at home and extended French military dominance abroad until he was defeated in 1815 and foreign armies occupied France. French politics were characterized thereafter by struggles for ascendancy among elite factions deeply distrustful of each other, and the struggles resulted in five regime downfalls during the next 150 years.

Finally, in Mexico after the second general strike of 1916 was smashed, an attempt to unify the numerous revolutionary leadership groups was made in the form of a new constitution containing provisions aimed at mollifying all important groups. But key leaders such as Zapata and Villa were not parties to the effort, and they remained disloyal to the new constitutional regime. A situation of attenuated government collapse continued and involved further elite bloodletting. Zapata was killed in April 1919, a key aide to Villa was assassinated later that year, and the Constitutionalist leaders, Carranza and Obregón, fell out with each other when Carranza nominated a stooge to replace him in the 1920 presidential election. Obregón then led a military revolt, and in May 1920 Carranza was killed while again fleeing to Vera Cruz. Obregón became president and set about constructing a more inclusive elite and regime structure, subordinating organized labor to the state, renegotiating ties with American and other foreign capitals in terms that were minimally acceptable to nationalist factions, and taking preliminary steps toward a program of land reform to placate peasant groups.

Yet, as evidenced by military revolts against Obregón's government in 1922 and 1923, by the assassination of Villa in 1923, and by the Cristero War of 1926–1929, which involved the repression of localized peasant uprisings encouraged by Church officials opposed to the federal state's takeover of educational institutions, reconfigured elites were clearly disunified. It took another crisis— the assassination of Obregón in July 1928 and its threat of renewed revolutionary strife—before what amounted to an elite settlement, engineered by Plutarco Calles in the months following Obregón's assassination, was negotiated (for an account, see Knight 1992). Thus, the Mexican revolution did not produce a new and hegemonic elite, although, as in the England case, fears of a revolutionary resurgence constituted an important incentive for an elite settlement some years later.

With the conspicuous addition of the Russian Revolution, discussed shortly, the English, French, and Mexican upheavals were the clearest instances of revolution in preindustrial societies and independent national states during the modern historical period. All three accorded broadly with the elite and non-elite preconditions, triggering crises, revolutionary intervals, and consequent elite outcomes specified earlier. I turn now to three revolutions that did produce new and hegemonic elites: the Russian, Italian, and German upheavals during and after World War I. I will argue that they were consistent with generalizations in chapter 1 about elites, non-elites, and politics. Those generalizations cast a somewhat new light on the three upheavals and why the outcome of each was a hegemonic, ideological unified elite.

REVOLUTION AND ELITE CIRCULATION

In 1914, disunified elites and unstable political regimes were evident in all European countries except Britain, Sweden, the Netherlands, and Switzerland, and this was the uniform pattern in Latin America and all other independent national states outside Europe, apart from Britain's former colonies in North America and the Antipodes. By 1914, moreover, national states in Western Europe, North America, and the Antipodes were industrial societies, while those in Eastern Europe and everywhere else (except Japan) were still preindustrial. Thus, at the start of World War I all independent national states satisfied the non-elite precondition for revolution: either a preindustrial or an industrial workforce configuration. But because of propitious home rule colonial circumstances and unifying struggles for independence or because of earlier elite settlements, a handful of national states (Britain, Sweden, the Netherlands, Switzerland, and the former British North American and Antipodean colonies) did not at the same time satisfy the elite precondition for revolution, namely, elite disunity.

The war that broke out in 1914 was a desperate struggle, and it greatly reduced economic well-being throughout Europe and much of the rest of the world. By the time it ended in 1918, sufficient damage had been done so that socialist elite factions and movements claiming to represent the working class and other downtrodden social categories were able to mount credible leveling threats to entrenched interests and established regimes in most European countries. However, it was only in Russia, Italy, and Germany that successful revolutions occurred, and in all three cases the outcome was a hegemonic, ideological unified elite. Why those countries and that outcome? Despite obvious disparities between them, not least in the makeup of their workforces (Russia was still preindustrial, but Italy, at least in its north, and Germany were industrial), it makes much sense to view the three revolutions as interconnected.

That elites in all three countries were disunified prior to World War I is readily seen. Like French elites during the eighteenth century, elites in Russia were split into two deeply opposed camps, the one defending absolutist monarchy and the customary status order, the other agitating for a parliamentary regime and various liberal reforms. Defeat in the 1904 war with Japan gave the liberal camp a momentary advantage and almost produced an overthrow of the absolutist monarchy in March 1905, but tactical concessions by the tsar, followed by ruthless repression, extended its life for a dozen years. In Italy and Germany, the consolidation of new national states during the last quarter of the nineteenth century involved deep conflicts among elites over the power of each country's monarchy and, in Italy, over the Church's place in the new national state. From the dates of national unification, important elite factions in Italy and Germany remained unreconciled to the forms that political institutions took and to the power that governing elites exerted through those institutions. Moreover, rapid industrialization soon created a large and actively hostile working class mobilized by leaders who proclaimed the coming of socialist revolution. By severely limiting the suffrage in Italy (to less than 5 percent of adult males), and in Germany by adopting placatory welfare measures as well as appealing to strong nationalist sentiments in recurrent foreign policy crises, governing elites were able to keep the lid on major civil strife prior to World War I.

The war was undoubtedly the crisis that triggered revolution in all three countries. The privations it caused in Russia sparked a multitude of peasant uprisings and military desertions that the tsarist regime was incapable of stemming. In March 1917, the regime collapsed when thousands of soldiers refused to fire on striking workers in Petrograd. A provisional government was established, but it lacked the support of the officer corps and it was unable to stem further peasant uprisings and industrial strikes, which were increasingly orchestrated through local soviets. A situation of government collapse spread.

In Italy, meanwhile, the war entailed devastating military losses that greatly enflamed domestic conflicts and eroded what remained of elite and non-elite support for established political institutions (Thompson 2008). As historian Martin Clark observed, "The Italians had been divided before, but by November 1918 they were more divided than ever—'combatants' against 'shirkers,' peasants against workers, patriots against defeatists. No conceivable form of government could suit them all" (1984, 200). The result was deadlock at the political level, with intransigent Socialist, Communist, Catholic, and Fascist Parties preventing the formation of governments capable of decisive action. Signaled by Gabriele D'Annunzio's fifteen-month insurgency in Fiume, by factory and land seizures, and by endemic strikes and riots, a collapse of public order seemed imminent.

In Germany, as in Russia, defeat in the war effectively destroyed the autocratic monarchical regime, discrediting the military and other elite groups associated with it. After Kaiser Wilhelm II's forced abdication in November 1918, a provisional government reluctantly headed by leaders of the Marxist and ostensibly revolutionary Social Democratic Party oversaw the transition to a new and thoroughly democratic Weimar Republic. However, the now ruling Social Democratic elites alienated many of their more vehement allies and supporters by forcibly suppressing several local uprisings that presaged a collapse of government authority, and by refusing to implement socialist measures for which there was no majority electoral support.

The Bolshevik seizure of power in Russia proved pivotal for all three countries because it suddenly made what had previously been a fanciful possibility—a socialist order on a national scale—brutally concrete. The Bolsheviks' consolidation of power during the first half of the 1920s demonstrated that socialism, in the sense of a matter-of-fact public ownership of the means of production, did not lead to immediate economic collapse. This spurred mobilizations of sizable portions of populations in industrial countries like northern Italy and Germany, whose members had much more to lose in a socialist revolution than "chains." Extremist antisocialist leaders soon came to head movements aimed at preventing such a revolution at any price and with any means. The victory of the Bolsheviks in Russia between 1917 and 1921 and their consolidation of power, together with the longstanding disunity of Italian and German elites and the damage done to Italy and Germany by World War I, are crucial for understanding the revolutionary upheavals that ensued in both countries.

What accounted for the Bolsheviks' victory? Certainly, there was nothing inevitable about it. As a result of peasant rebellions, a consequent inability to secure enough grain to avoid drastic food price inflation, and a drumbeat of factory strikes and military mutinies, including an attempted military coup in August 1917, the provisional government that replaced the tsarist regime was broken by November of that year. Tiny Bolshevik groups in Petrograd and Moscow then simply took power in bloodless coups that went virtually unnoticed by ordinary Russians. Acting in accordance with their self-conception of being a "vanguard" force that would incrementally move Russian society toward a socialist utopia, Lenin and his associates maneuvered secretly and ruthlessly during the winter months of 1917–1918 to eliminate rival factions by forming and deploying the Bolshevik security agency, the Cheka, against them, disbanding the newly elected Constituent Assembly by force in early January, suing for peace with Germany two months later, and building a Red Army with which to prosecute a far-flung civil war against sundry enemies from within and without the country.

The struggle's extensiveness and the extreme ideological polarization it created prevented moderate forces from making significant headway. The result, in 1920, was Bolshevik victory on the battlefield, although it was due as much to nationalist uprisings in territories controlled by anti-Bolshevik forces as to Bolshevik military prowess. It remained for Lenin and his clique to achieve dominance of the socialist camp by crushing the Kronstadt naval mutiny in March 1921 while simultaneously inducing their party's Congress to abdicate its power over the Central Committee, which Lenin and his cronies controlled. A highly centralized elite structure and a regime without meaningful checks or counterweights were consolidated during the next several years. By 1925–1926 at the latest—after Stalin had succeeded Lenin and stripped Zinoviev, Trotsky, and other rivals of their government positions—one could speak of Russia being in the grip of a new hegemonic and ideological unified elite. The extensiveness of government collapse between 1917 and 1921, combined with the Bolsheviks' cogent and instrumental version of Marxism, enabled them to prevail.

Neither was there anything inevitable about the occurrence of revolution in northern Italy and Germany after World War I. Their industrial non-elite workforce configurations probably made both countries immune to an egalitarian leveling revolution fueled by a large and landless peasantry. By 1920, farmers constituted less than half of the German workforce, most of them being small landowners as the term "farmer" denotes, and the numerous Catholics among them were firmly anchored in the moderate Center Party. In 1921, Italy as a whole had a much larger body of agricultural and artisan workers—perhaps two-thirds of its workforce—but they were most numerous in the south where the conservative, antirevolutionary political influence of the Church was strongest. In addition, depopulation of the countryside as a result of northern industrialization and large-scale emigration abroad, together with the inflation-driven prosperity that World War I created in rural Italy, had doubled the number of peasant landowners during the preceding ten years, with, for example, 30 to 40 percent of rural heads of families in the south owning land by 1921 (Clark 1984, 209).

Thus, the non-elite precondition for a leveling revolution—a preindustrial workforce consisting mainly of impoverished and landless peasants—no longer existed in Italy or Germany after World War I. Instead when the threat of leveling revolution posed by socialist and communist leaders, who mobilized the large urban working class in each country, became stark, masses of rural voters in central and northern Italy and in Germany's Protestant north joined with sizable parts of the middle and upper middle classes to support virulently antisocialist Fascist and Nazi Parties respectively (Hamilton 1982; Paxton 2004). The result was broad cross-class support for movements that promised to prevent a leveling revolution, by force if necessary.

Although the non-elite configuration characteristic of industrial societies underlay the antileveling revolutions that took place in Italy and Germany, this was by no means the whole story. One must also consider the configuration of elites and the impact of World War I and the Russian revolution on both countries. Conflicts within disunified elites in Italy and Germany were greatly enflamed by the war. First, Italy's belated entry into it, in May 1915, was extremely divisive: key leaders like Giovanni Giolitti made many elite enemies while maneuvering unsuccessfully to keep Italy neutral, the Socialist Party elite faction refused to abandon its "internationalist" principles and join the war effort, and demagogues such as D'Annunzio and Mussolini agitated for war and denounced other elite persons and factions as cowardly and unpatriotic (Thompson 2008, 39–60). After Italy's bruising military defeat at Caporetto late in 1917, a *Fascio* of prowar Nationalists and Liberals formed to counter "defeatist" elites, while numerous *fasci*, some of which soon constituted the core of Mussolini's movement, simultaneously emerged among local elites. The residue of this heightened conflict, once the war ended, was increased elite distrust and intransigence on all sides. An electoral earthquake resulting from the implementation of universal male suffrage and proportional representation in the 1919 parliamentary election further dissolved any basis for a strong government so that, by 1921, there could only be "a series of short-lived coalitions under weak premiers, living from hand to mouth as public order collapsed" (Clark 1984, 213).

In Germany, the outbreak of World War I had brought a temporary civil truce between all main elite factions, including the avowedly revolutionary Social Democrats. But by late 1916, under the weight of increasing domestic hardship and political disagreement, a military dictatorship was, in effect, created. Military setbacks two years later triggered the regime's downfall, proclamation of a republic at Weimar, and a brief period of civil warfare involving several leftist uprisings and their forcible suppression. Military leaders and other right-wing elite persons were discredited but claimed that defeat in the war was due to left-wing sabotage. Left-wing elites were badly split between intransigent communist revolutionaries and more moderate democratic socialists. The Weimar Republic was unsupported by anything like a unified front of elites from its outset in 1919, as was immediately apparent in further left-wing uprisings and an attempted right-wing coup in March 1920. During the next ten years, in a process that has been extensively investigated and described by scholars (for example, Hamilton 1982; Evans 2003; Paxton 2004), centrist elites and parties steadily lost influence and electoral support to radical leaders and parties on the left and right. By 1930, parliamentary majorities supporting positive government actions could no longer be fashioned, and rule by presidential decree became the norm.

Situations of government paralysis and collapse developed in both countries and constituted the conditions in which the Mussolini and Hitler movements were able to gain power. The Italian and German governments could not or would not prevent paramilitary forces of the most extreme parties and movements, especially those of the far right, from controlling many localities and from intimidating or killing their opponents. During 1921–1922 in Italy, Socialist- and Communist-dominated working-class sections of northern cities were in open revolt, and this created the specter of an imminent leveling revolution that would duplicate the one in Russia. In reaction, Fascist strong-arm squads, who often received arms, ammunition, and other support from the military and police, took over town after town in Italy's Po River Valley and industrialized north. De facto control of such important areas gave Mussolini the trump card he needed to extract a summons from the king to form a government in October 1922. A year later in Germany, after failing ignominiously in his Munich *putsch* to duplicate Mussolini's success, Hitler and the National Socialist Workers Party (NSDAP) began to deploy paramilitary forces to intimidate opponents, often with the connivance of military and police officers as well as the judiciary. As the size and aggressiveness of *Sturmabteilungen* (SA Brown Shirts) grew during the 1920s, government paralysis and collapse became increasingly widespread, although it never equaled the extensiveness of the Italian condition in 1921–1922.

Hitler and the NSDAP thus lacked the ability to force their way into power and had to engage, instead, in a protracted electoral struggle, in which the effectiveness of their paramilitary units and party

cadres—their "organizational weapon"—together with shrill promises to crush Marxism and "Bolshevism," absolve farmers of their
debts, and expunge treasonous Jews and others who were accused of
preventing Germany's return to national greatness made Hitler and
the NSDAP the pivotal element in politics after 1930. By winning
overwhelming majorities in northern Protestant farming communities and attracting large numbers of mainly Protestant voters in the
middle and upper middle classes frightened by the seeming strength
of the left and at the same time disillusioned with established conservative parties, the NSDAP became the largest party, capturing more
than a third of the popular vote in 1932. That put Hitler in position
to demand the chancellorship, and, after intrigues within a clique
of conservative leaders around the president, Hindenburg, he was
appointed chancellor on January 30, 1933.

What role did ideology play in bringing the two antisocialist movements to power? Despite promises to implement new and distinctive
ways of structuring industrial societies that amounted to a corporat-
ist ideology, the Fascist and Nazi programs were basically reactive.
They were against socialism and against the democratic institutions
and processes that many socialists claimed would ultimately help
usher in a socialist society. In effect, socialists, and antisocialists
alike credited Marx's prophecy that capitalist industrial societies
would necessarily produce a majority of proletarian victims whose
sheer numbers would enable them to take over politically. Because
experience with the workforce trajectories and political dynamics
of industrial societies was at the time quite limited, this was a plausible outlook. In no industrial capitalist society had the proportion
of alienated and actively hostile manual industrial workers yet lev-
eled off or begun to decline, as eventually happened when societies moved toward a postindustrial workforce configuration. What
socialists and antisocialists disagreed most deeply about, therefore,
were the consequences of an eventual socialist victory, with the former expecting it to produce some more or less utopian social order
and the latter expecting that it would quickly lead to a general retrogression in material conditions and their own degradation.

For those who saw themselves as underdogs, or who sympathized
with underdogs, socialism was to be eagerly anticipated. But for

those who were situated in the large and generally better-off strata of northern Italy and Germany or who had, like many former peasants in both countries, only recently become propertied, socialism was to be feared and resisted. Taken together, better-off middle- and upper-middle-class persons plus small propertied former peasants and artisans outnumbered the manual industrial working class, and enough of them could be mobilized with the use of antisocialist appeals by unscrupulous political adventurers like Mussolini and Hitler to carry the day. In short, Fascist-Nazi ideology was a mirror image of revolutionary socialism, and its compelling character rose most directly from what had just transpired in Russia.

In Germany, a fundamental change in elite composition and functioning was apparent within eighteen months of Hitler's accession to the chancellorship. A Reichstag fire, followed by a rigged election in March 1933, provided the wherewithal to ram provisions through the Reichstag that enabled Hitler to rule by decree. He soon abolished state parliaments, suppressed trade unions, and outlawed all parties other than the NSDAP. At the end of June 1934, he had Ernst Röhm and two hundred SA and opposition leaders murdered to gain military support for merging the offices of chancellor and president in his person following the death of Hindenberg in August of that year. From August 1934 at the latest, a hegemonic elite was in substantial control of Germany, though it had to propitiate the business elite as well as restless NSDAP factions until waging total war in 1942 further radicalized the Nazi elite and made it utterly dominant (Paxton 2004, 141–58).

In Italy, by contrast, the Fascist consolidation of power took longer and always remained somewhat incomplete. After forming a government in November 1922, Mussolini kept Fascist *squadristi* intact, but he made no strong moves to liquidate opponents and monopolize power. Elections were held under an amended but widely accepted electoral law in April 1924, and the Fascist-led bloc emerged with two-thirds of the vote. When Giacomo Matteotti, the new Socialist Party leader, denounced the elections as involving intimidation and fraud, he was assassinated by six Fascist squadristi, probably with Mussolini's approval. But instead of using the assassination to mount a full-scale parliamentary assault on Mussolini's government, Socialists, Communists, and other elites opposing Mussolini boycotted parliament and gave him important breathing space. It was not until 1925–1926 that Mussolini and the Fascist elite began a systematic suppression of rival elite persons and groups inside and outside parliament, and it was only after a fourth attempt to assassinate Mussolini, in 1926, that they began to insist on the political conformity and centralization of decision-making networks that are hallmarks of an ideological unified elite. Even then, important elite persons, such as senior leaders of the military, the Church, some portions of the civil service, and some members of the Senate, were not "fascistized" in any thorough way. Indeed, the Fascist Party itself became more an appendage of the Mussolini government than its central organizing unit (Paxton 2004, 124–25). Nevertheless, the substantial transformation of political institutions and the subordination of all other elites to an autocratic state, in which Mussolini's word was law, gave the Italian upheaval and outcome a revolutionary texture.

To summarize, revolutionary elite circulations in Russia, Italy, and Germany were interconnected. All three occurred in societies that satisfied the elite and non-elite preconditions for revolution, although the circulations depended crucially on (1) the catastrophic impact of World War I on the three countries and (2) the concatenating effects of the Russian Revolution on industrialized Italy and Germany. As the crucial event in this sequence, the Russian Revolution was virtually unique in the modern historical period. Although a few leveling revolutions in preindustrial societies had occurred previously (for example, the English, French, and Mexican Revolutions), the Russian Revolution was the first to produce a lasting new and ideological unified elite. The unparalleled crisis that World War I constituted for the tsarist regime, the resulting extensiveness of government collapse between 1917 and 1921, and the instrumentally detailed character of Bolshevik ideology help account for this singular outcome. In turn, the impact of the Russian Revolution and its outcome on war-devastated Italy and Germany, in both of which elites were badly disunified, was immense. By giving the idea of socialist revolution practical credibility and thus inspiring leftist elite factions while terrifying right-wing ones, the Russian

Revolution was the most proximate cause of antileveling Fascist and Nazi revolutions in Italy and Germany, respectively.

ELITES, NON-ELITES, AND REVOLUTION SINCE WORLD WAR II

Of the three ideological unified elites created during the twentieth century's interwar period, only the Russian-Soviet elite survived World War II. During the quarter century that followed, it imposed by military force or inspired ideologically and encouraged with military assistance clones in countries located around the Soviet Union's perimeter and at greater distances from it: Yugoslavia and Albania immediately following the war, Eastern Europe between 1947 and 1949, North Korea between 1946 and 1948, China in 1948–1949, North Vietnam in 1954, Cuba in 1960–1961, South Yemen in 1970, and Cambodia and Afghanistan for brief periods after 1975. From the dates indicated, all those countries had ruling elites patterned recognizably on the Soviet model and claiming to be revolutionary in the Soviet sense. In reality, none originated in a revolution comparable to the Russian upheaval or consistent with the conception of revolution here.

The clones were created in quite different ways: through Soviet military conquest or regional hegemony, through military victory in organized and protracted civil wars or anticolonial wars of national liberation, or through political subterfuge. Not originating in an indigenous, full-blown revolution of the Russian kind, the ideological coherence and unity of the elite in each of the clones was more fragile than in the Soviet elite. In Eastern Europe, for example, struggles between "nativist" and "Moscovite" elite factions were persistent, and the dominance of Moscovite factions depended heavily on the presence or proximity of Soviet military force. Elsewhere—in Albania, North Korea, North Vietnam, and Cuba—cults of personality centered on a founding leader were crucial to maintaining rough approximations of the Soviet model. In Yugoslavia, as noted in chapter 1, elites led by Josip Broz Tito proved unable to contain the clashing ethnic identities and economic interests of the six constituent republics, and after Tito's death in 1980, Yugoslavia disintegrated violently little more than ten years later.

The People's Republic of China (PRC) was a complicated exception. Its communist elite and regime have been thought by Western scholars to have originated in a revolution that occurred during all or most of the period between 1911 and 1949 (for example, Skocpol 1979). However, protracted civil warfare waged by an array of warlords and forces comprising a deeply disunified, chaotic set of elites—in which Chiang Kai-shek's Kuomintang leaders and Communist Party (CCP) leaders were the most important protagonists—is a more accurate political depiction of China during those four tumultuous decades. It was only after the CCP achieved victory on the battlefield in 1948–1949 and installed itself in Beijing that a revolution in the present sense of the term eventually occurred. It took the CCP and its regime several years to gain control of territory south of the Yangtze River, which it had not controlled when fighting Chiang Kai-shek's forces. This entailed considerable internal elite conflict, as evidenced by the Hundred Flowers Campaign and an Anti-Rightist backlash during the mid-1950s. After the debacle of the Great Leap Forward, 1958–1960, in which twenty to thirty million people perished from hunger, factional intrigues, carefully hidden from public view, deepened (Fairbank 1986, 296–314).

Between 1966 and 1968 internal elite conflict exploded in the paroxysm of the Great Proletarian Cultural Revolution, which was instigated by Mao Zedong and his "anti-elitist" faction to extirpate "bourgeois" bureaucrats and "capitalist roaders" of the kind that Mao believed had taken control of the Soviet Union after Nikita Khrushchev's denunciation of Stalin in 1956. Spearheaded by university and other mostly youthful activists, a leveling revolution, the kaleidoscopic complexity of which defies brief encapsulation, got underway (see monumental histories of the Cultural Revolution by Macfarquhar and Schoenhals [2006] and Yang Jisheng [2016/2021]). Its intensity varied between provinces, counties, districts, and municipalities and between units of revolutionaries, but it is estimated that upward of one and a half million government officials, teachers, and civilians of many kinds were killed, often in gruesome ways (Yang 2016/2021, 345–64; Mishra 2021).

Eventually recognizing that the revolution he and his faction had instigated was out of control, Mao asked the still-intact People's Liberation Army to disband the Red Guard and other revolutionary groups. Nevertheless, leveling actions continued until the Fourth National People's Congress, held in complete secrecy in January 1975, at which Deng Xiaoping and a "pragmatist" faction in the CCP elite became ascendant. At the last Politburo meeting over which he presided, in May 1975, Mao put Deng in charge of overall government operations (Yang 2016/2021, 496–500). Deng and his faction ended the revolutionary interval by restoring order and beginning to repair its economic damage.

Mao died in September 1976. A month later, in what amounted to a coup dramatically recounted by Yang (2016/2021, 568–84), the Gang of Four, one of whom was Mao's radical and erstwhile wife, Jiang Qing, were arrested and publicly humiliated. Factional clashes over the extent and wisdom of economic and political reforms instituted by Deng continued and culminated in the Tiananmen Square massacre of student demonstrators and nearly open elite warfare in 1989. Since Tiananmen, the pragmatist elite faction, currently led by Xi Jinping, have presided over China's miraculous economic development.

The absence of a revolutionary origin of the ideological unified elite in Cuba was obvious. In 1959, Fidel Castro and his associates gained power in circumstances that exhibited almost none of the preconditions and features associated with a leveling revolution, which they only later claimed to have carried out. By the 1950s, and probably since the 1930s when American military occupation of Cuba ended, the country's non-elite workforce configuration was that of an early industrial rather than a preindustrial society. It was in that respect more susceptible to an antileveling than a leveling revolution. Cuban elites had long been disunified, with the faction headed by Fulgencio Batista, a former army sergeant, in dictatorial control for most of the period between the American withdrawal and the Castro forces' victory at the end of 1958. No major crisis collapsed the Batista regime and no revolutionary interval ensued when Batista was forced to leave the country late in 1958 in the face of military and business elites' demands for his departure.

During their three-year insurgency, based in Cuba's mountains, the Castro forces articulated no ideology more cogent than vague populist and reformist promises that had a Robin Hood flavor. In a memorable phrase, Theodore Draper observed that the so-called Cuban Revolution involved "a leader in search of a movement, a movement in search of power, and power in search of an ideology" (1965, 132–33). Castro and his guerrilla fighters presented themselves as something quite different from the ideological unified elite they turned out to be once government and military control enabled them to impose drastic changes on Cuban society "from above." Because the non-elite precondition for a leveling revolution was absent, subterfuge was, presumably, the only way in which an elite that subsequently announced leveling aims could obtain power. In any event, until age and illness forced Castro to step aside in 2007, Cuban elite unity was primarily a one-man show. Its persistence without Castro and, latterly, without his younger brother Raúl, who stepped down as Communist Party leader, together with departures from the Politburo and Central Committee of all five surviving veterans of the early Castro years in April 2021, will be precarious.

The implication is that, of the several elites claiming to be products of revolution, probably only the Soviet elite's claim withstands close scrutiny, and it is gone. Although the Soviet elite had clones, their significantly different origins everywhere resulted in less comprehensive, more personality-centered variants. What has been the fate of these clones?

In China and Vietnam, Communist Party control has been relaxed, although by no means abolished, and corruption has spread. On the other hand, relaxed Party control, enormous reservoirs of cheap labor, and success in obtaining foreign investment capital have made the Chinese and Vietnamese trajectories the opposite of the Soviet Union's. Economic growth has been strong, sizable middle classes have emerged, and gigantic industrialization and infrastructure projects have absorbed much surplus peasant labor into urban workforces and broadly better living conditions. It is a well-known postulate of social science that these socioeconomic trends will ultimately be incompatible with the persistence of revolutionary elites: either their centralized control will stifle economic progress and create a crisis greater than Tiananmen in 1989, or continued growth of middle classes and further social differentiation will slowly break the elites apart.

However, this either/or scenario may be misleading in twenty-first-century conditions. It captures well enough what has happened so far in North Korea, where the ruling elite has been unable to prevent famine-like conditions, and to a lesser extent in Cuba or Iran, where elites professing a single ideology or doctrine of religion have retarded economic development substantially. But the scenario is less obviously applicable to China and Vietnam, where development has been dynamic and prospering middle classes have emerged without breaking the hold of Communist Party elites on power. State socialism has been emptied of meaning in both countries, but their elites stoke nationalism as a replacement. Nationalism with a strongly anti-American thrust was a mobilization strategy to which Fidel Castro and Cuban elites long resorted, and it is an important tool that senior clerics in Iran employ to retain their grip on power despite periodic mass protests and crippling international economic sanctions.

There are additional reasons to doubt that an either/or scenario forecasts the fate of ideological unified elites in twenty-first-century conditions. A learning curve is one reason. Having observed the Soviet elite's demise, Chinese, Vietnamese, and perhaps even Iranian elites are on heightened alert against choices and actions that might bring disintegration. It is also conceivable that the postulate of an inverse relationship between strong economic development and the persistence of professedly revolutionary elites is weakened, if not negated, in conditions that enable such elites to couple economic expansion with continued political repression. This is accomplished by dramatically increasing the provision of public goods—transportation, health care, basic education, national defense, increased mass leisure and entertainment—while clamping down on coordination goods—political rights, civil liberties and human rights, unregulated mass media and the Internet, access to higher education—that enable potential opponents to mobilize but are less critical for economic expansion (De Mesquita and Downs 2005). However, the government of semi-autonomous Hong Kong appeared unable to do both, and it is an open question if the PRC government can accomplish both in Hong Kong after having stripped it of political autonomy. The handful of ideological unified elites that currently exist face daunting challenges: absorbing large and essentially surplus rural dwellers into urban workforces; problems of environmental pollution, global warming, and water shortages; dwindling petroleum and other energy resources required for economic growth; and the COVID-19 and other potentially deadly pandemics. Disintegrations like that of the Soviet elite can hardly be ruled out. Yet in the changed and changing circumstances of the twenty-first century, ideological unified elites have advantages that the Soviet elite did not have or was too ossified to seize.

CONCLUDING OBSERVATIONS

I have tried to draw out implications of chapter 1's generalizations about elites, non-elites, and politics for the origins, processes, and consequences of revolution. My thesis has been that revolution occurs only when deep elite disunity intersects with a preindustrial or industrial non-elite configuration. Even then, its occurrence requires an extraordinary political crisis or gross ineptitude by ruling elites. Societies in which elites are consensual unified and/or have postindustrial non-elite configurations are immune to revolution. Revolution is not the recurrent, cyclical phenomenon that Pareto theorized (see Finer 1966; Femia 2007); it is, instead, a rare and highly contingent paroxysm that can occur in just two phases of socioeconomic development.

I offer two relatively novel conclusions. The first is that antileveling fascist revolutions are probably best viewed as peculiar to the circumstances of a few industrialized capitalist societies in interwar Europe with deeply disunified elites. In them, the new and unfamiliar industrial configuration of non-elites led many people to believe that alienated manual industrial workers and their families would soon constitute a majority. Combined with the abruptly increased credibility that radical socialist programs had after the Russian Revolution, the prospect of leveling revolution seemed real. It instilled panic in large categories of generally better-off bureaucratic, service, and somewhat propertied agricultural and artisan personnel. Where, as in Italy and Germany, elite factions were at each other's throats and prepared to mobilize pro- and antileveling segments of non-elites by disseminating extremist doctrines, and where the social and economic consequences of World War I were especially dire, fascist revolutions occurred, albeit not completely in Italy, and in Germany mainly when the Nazi regime struggled to wage total war. As Robert Paxton observed in his authoritative *The Anatomy of Fascism*, "Adequate space was not available for fascism until after World War I and the Bolshevik Revolution. Fascist movements could first reach full development only in the outwash from those two tidal waves" (2004, 172). But chances that deep elite disunity, a non-elite industrial configuration, and a set of contingencies analogous to those following World War I might recur are vanishingly small. This suggests that fascist revolutions "from above" should probably not constitute a general category in the study of revolution.

My second conclusion is a corollary of the first. The Russian Revolution was a seminal but wholly unique event. Its outcome—the victory and consolidation of an ideological unified elite—depended on circumstances that have not attended the rise of a similar elite anywhere else to the same degree. One should, therefore, be cautious about inferring general dynamics and patterns from the Russian Revolution and its elite outcome. Broad inferences about Russian-like revolutionary elites and a "revolutionary route to modernity," such as Barrington Moore Jr. (1966) and like-minded believers in the efficacy of revolution have postulated, do not stand up in at least two respects. First, beyond the Russian case it is difficult to find clear empirical referents for such inferences. Instigated by Mao Zedong and his ruling clique in a preindustrial society, the Great Proletarian Cultural Revolution in China was a catastrophe for modernization. Second, disintegration of the Soviet elite, together with conspicuous changes that have since occurred in the Chinese, Vietnamese, Cuban, and Iranian elites, strongly suggests that ideological unified elites are not capable of lasting in pristine form beyond two or three generations.

Does revolution bring political improvement? From the standpoint of political realism, the answer must be an emphatic "No." Because of the searing and lasting enmities revolution creates, it never eventuates in an elite that is consensually unified. Its consequence is either a still more disunified or an ideologically unified elite. Neither is congenial to a vibrant society. Although much is heard from persons outraged by what they regard as fundamental moral deficiencies in today's political regimes, not least Western democracies, the sweeping "revolutionary" changes that these persons sometimes demand are just dreams and wishful thoughts that are deeply imprudent. It is appropriate to close with Napoleon's reflection about revolution when in exile on St. Helena, as recorded by his secretary: "Revolution is one of the greatest ills with which the heavens can afflict the earth. It is the scourge of the generation that makes it; any gains it procures cannot offset the distress it spreads through life. It enriches the poor, who are not satisfied; it impoverishes the rich, who will never forget it. It overturns everything, makes everyone unhappy, and procures happiness for nobody" (Cohen 2021 on the two-hundredth anniversary of Napoleon's death).

Chapter Three

Elites, Non-Elites, and Democracy

Conceiving of democracy as a solution for many of the world's problems has been a widespread practice in Western countries during recent decades. Democracy has deep ideological roots in the West, although as a term it did not figure greatly in popular discourse until after World War I, when it amounted to a rationalization of representative political practices that elites had instituted gradually and piecemeal during the preceding half-century. The interwar period in Europe involved the downfalls of more than a dozen unstable, more or less "democratic" regimes that various factions in disunified elites managed to install in the wake of World War I (Linz and Stepan 1978; Huntington 1991, 13–26). It was only after elites in liberal Western countries hailed victory in World War II as "the triumph of democracy" that the term became utterly dominant in political discourse. Following that war and in a Cold War context, democracy was enshrined as the cardinal feature of Western countries comprising "the free world." Liberations of colonies outside the West during postwar decades were seen as betokening democracy's global spread, apart from the bloc of communist countries.

DEMOCRACY PROMOTION

During the 1950s and 1960s many affluent, educated, and semi-leisured Westerners embraced democracy as a solution to ills they discerned at home and abroad. Their embrace underpinned measures and programs designed to improve the life chances of people from poorer backgrounds, and it provided the rationale for many efforts at educational reform, such as preschool learning programs and large increases in the number of university places for graduates of secondary schools. In the United States, the civil rights movement, which arose during the 1950s among African Americans in the South and their sympathizers in the North, rapidly received elite endorsement. The movement prevailed sufficiently to suggest the prospect of a large segment of the American population that had been almost totally excluded from careers, leading to middle-class statuses becoming equal or even privileged contenders for those statuses. Women as well as various groups suffering discriminations soon moved into the foreground and demanded rectification of their situations. Because of the United States's premier global position, the American movements and policies resulting from them came to be viewed as models for what should be done in other countries.

The 1960s were a decade during which utopian radicalism and a profession of sturdy moral principles, regardless of circumstances, were prevalent, especially among university students. In addition to the major student-led uprising in France in May 1968, serious disturbances brought about by bodies of radical students occurred in virtually every Western society. University buildings were seized, administrative files were rifled, and radical political demands were shouted. It was difficult to negotiate with student protesters because their egalitarian principles left them without stable organization and leadership. Moreover, the optimism of professed elite sentiment prevented clear-cut confrontations between adults and students or between extreme and less extreme positions. It was obvious that the educated and informed parts of Western publics as well as their political leaders wanted to believe that differences between them and protesting students were mainly matters of maturity and discretion. Most elite persons and informed adults sought to respect publicly the goals proclaimed by student radicals.

From an exposure to student radicalism and mass media reporting of it, one could hardly have concluded that in political reality the interests of people frequently differ and that people, if they can, pursue their own interests as they see them. The lack of political realism among student radicals and the influence they exerted on public consciousness left most actual issues and prospects unaddressed. Once the radicals and students influenced by them finished university educations and moved into government and academic positions and many jobs in media and entertainment industries, it was inevitable that young scholars, civil servants, media personalities, entertainers, writers, and rising politicians would hold more extreme views of desirable social reforms than had generally been prevalent before the 1960s.

These are reasons why democracy came to be pursued with unalloyed enthusiasm by Western countries during the twentieth century's final quarter. Democracy was invoked as the remedy for nearly all that was wrong in the world. Autocratic and corrupt regimes, which were usually controlled overtly or covertly by military elites, were regarded as preventing or retarding economic and political development. They could be swept aside if populations suffering under them opted for democracy and the freedoms and institutions that Western elites and educated publics sentimentally portrayed as principal reasons for their own countries' historical triumphs. A more realistic view would have seen these attributes as in considerable measure artifacts of Western domination and exploitation of much of the world during modern history. In any event, it was widely believed that promoting democracy would liberate oppressed populations and in time lessen their hostility toward the West.

Western political leaders, pundits, scholars, and others agreed that the behaviors and configurations of elites and regimes in most non-Western countries were not propitious for democracy. Prevailingly, they advocated replacing them with persons, groups, and regimes more responsive to the supposed democratic sentiments of impoverished non-elite publics. How an ostensible "wave" of democratization had accompanied the independence of many former colonies during the 1950s and early 1960s, only to be rolled back by a "reverse wave" during and after the late 1960s, was highlighted and studied (for example, Huntington 1991). The autocratic Portuguese regime's overthrow in 1974, principally by junior military officers disheartened by the counterinsurgency warfare necessary to retain control of the Angola, Portuguese Guinea, and Mozambique colonies, was seen as presaging a new and more sweeping "third wave" of democratization outside the West. As two distinguished scholars, Juan Linz and Alfred Stepan, put it, democracy was coming to be "the only game in town" (1996; see also Diamond 2008).

Even conservative elite factions and governments in the United States, Britain, and other Western countries were vocal proponents of this view (Gordon 2020). That democracy as a concept and term in Western political discourse had historically been primarily a post-hoc rationalization of representative practices gradually adopted by elites was ignored. That *stable* representative democratic regimes in the West, whatever their limitations historically, had depended first and foremost on elites concluding that representative practices posed no lethal threat to their diverse and conflicting self-interests was a proposition too heinous to entertain.

Western think-tanks and government agencies dutifully kept track of authoritarian regime downfalls and the incidence of freely competitive elections in non-Western countries. Western governments, private foundations, and nongovernmental organizations allocated large sums of money to tutoring pro-democracy activists in those countries in the principles and techniques of democratic governance. It is fair to say, nonetheless, that during the twentieth century's final quarter and the twenty-first century's initial two decades, few stable democratic political systems resulted from those efforts. Political events and patterns in countries outside the West generally ran counter to democracy. Measures of democratic freedoms registered steady declines, while failed or failing states increased in number. Evidence of rigged elections, controlled media, endemic corruption, and numerous other practices at odds with democracy mounted (for example, Kurlantzick 2013; Mounk 2021).

Overthrows of a rigidly theocratic regime in Afghanistan in 2001 and a tyrannical secular regime in Iraq in 2003 by U.S. and allied military forces ignited vicious insurgencies led by deposed elites, with Afghanistan's return to theocratic rule and Iraq's territorial disintegration being probable. The toppling of a despotic regime in Ukraine by mass protests during 2003 ushered in a pervasively corrupt government. After a second uprising drove that government from power and Russia took control of Crimea in early 2014 and supported rebellious militias in the eastern Donbas region, Ukraine's lasting division along the cultural "fault line" separating its eastern and western parts seemed likely (Huntington 1996, 17).

During the "Arab Spring" of 2011, which is appraised in chapter 5, uprisings by masses of people, many of whom were imbued with Western urgings to "choose democracy," helped unseat repressive military regimes in Tunisia, Egypt, and Libya and sparked an emulative uprising against autocratic rule in Syria. Except in Tunisia, the uprisings, which were greeted ecstatically by democracy enthusiasts in the West, soon had unsavory consequences: a military coup and still more repressive regime in Egypt, descent into virtual anarchy in Libya, horrific civil warfare in Syria from which no democratic regime could possibly emerge, and the rise of a savage chiliastic movement vowing to recreate the Caliphate of early Islam and annihilate Westerners for their alleged iniquities.

Prospects for spreading democracy throughout the world, which were always more imaginary than real, receded. It is noteworthy that in one of his first policy statements as U.S. secretary of state in the Biden administration, Antony Blinken announced, "We will not promote democracy through costly military interventions or by attempting to overthrow authoritarian regimes by force. We have tried these tactics in the past. However well intentioned, they haven't worked" (U.S. Department of State 2021).

ELITES AND DEMOCRACY

Although one's personal preference may be for democratic politics, one need not believe that in most countries and circumstances the democratic ideal can be closely approached. Meaningfully democratic institutions and practices depend on which of the four kinds of elites a society has. Obviously, *no kind* is compatible with the democratic ideal. Worse, only *two kinds* are reasonably compatible with the practical and limited form of democracy now practiced in Western and a few non-Western countries. Finally, *neither* of these two kinds is reliably conducive to even a limited embodiment of the democratic ideal.

The most common kind of political regime, in which elites are disunified, has the basic feature of institutional instability. While institutions operated by some part of a disunified elite may at times have a formally democratic façade, the institutions are hardly worth much promotion or defense because they are unlikely to survive a serious political crisis. Typically, any substantial increase in normal political tensions leads, with or without a military coup, to a more repressive regime. Although that regime may eventually mellow or even be replaced by a more democratic one with the tacit consent of the veto group associated with the military, the improvement is likely to be merely an interval in a succession of repressive regimes. As highlighted in chapter 1, historical evidence is overwhelming that disunified elites and unstable institutions persist through most vicissitudes and each new regime must in practice be one permitted by those who happen to control military forces.

The circumstances in which, on rare occasions, disunified elites become ideologically, consensually, or imperfectly unified are not likely to appeal to democratic sentiments and do not lead reliably to regimes that would be widely regarded as democratic. An ideologically unified elite does not allow competitive politics, and where it exists meaningful actions motivated by democratic sentiments are nearly impossible. An imperfectly unified elite allows institutions that satisfy most criteria for practical democracy, yet for a considerable part of elites and voters—the part that regularly loses in elections—democratic shortcomings will seem extreme. Those who most like to consider themselves genuine democrats find that they are consistently in the minority, while more conservative and traditional persons who are part of the majority are inclined, perhaps cynically, to be "democrats in spite of themselves." However, an imperfectly unified elite may evolve into a consensually unified elite, which happened in Japan, France, and a few other countries during the twentieth century's final quarter. That clears the way for a more widely accepted practical democracy, but the evolution depends on socially radical groups becoming disillusioned with their democratic ideals.

Of the four kinds of elites, consensually unified elites are clearly most compatible with criteria for practical democracy. Yet a regime operated by this kind of elite need not necessarily be democratic. It can be based, as it was in most historical cases, on a highly restricted suffrage or, as has long been the case in parts of the United States, systematic voter suppression. Even temporary dictatorship or the dominance of a high-handed chief executive, such as Donald Trump, is possible so long as elites remain internally trusting and prepared to cooperate in defeating or otherwise removing the chief executive if he or she proves to be seriously incompetent or incapacitated.

Practical democracy that lasts depends, fundamentally, on the ability of consensual unified elites to keep political tensions limited. Where such elites do this, the problem for people imbued with democratic ideals is deciding how much agitation they should try to center on issues they consider morally right but are also potentially explosive. The champions of such issues are likely to find that members of consensual unified elites distort, partially suppress, or simply confuse such issues if doing so seems necessary to maintain institutional stability. Morally charged issues will be subject to "benign neglect," for instance, when and if a large portion of a consensually unified elite concludes that previous handling has brought the issues to a threshold of articulation and antagonism beyond which stability will be endangered.

Should those who cannot get the hearing they think their moral causes deserve acquiesce to such treatment by elites? If it is correct that consensual unified elites are ordinarily quite capable of managing political tensions, the question is without significance. Suppose, however, that elites cannot quite do this in the face of massive public demonstrations, dark portrayals of them spread through social media, or some economic, environmental, or public health catastrophe. This would terminate consensual elite unity and create a disunified elite with the usual consequence of military control and suppression of political protest in times of crisis.

From the standpoint of political realism, a mature and experienced advocate of democracy must always settle for a political order that is considerably less than ideal. Elites that are consensually unified, or approach being so, are necessary for practical democracy that is durable. Only such elites will effectively manage issues whose open and dogmatic expression would create unchecked conflict. Where elites do this over the course of many years, representative institutions guided by reasonably competitive and influential elections are possible, although not inevitable. Where, conversely, elites fully and openly express the views of conflicting interests, then at some point political freedom for considerable numbers of elite and non-elite persons will have to be suppressed or the polity will not survive.

This negates the fashionable, but fatuous, notion that the most democratic, and therefore most desirable, political system is one in which the myriad interests and identities in a large population are clearly represented and articulated at the elite level. The posing of "real choices" in practical democratic systems always threatens to weaken elite unity and undermine political stability. The person who recognizes this cannot accept an absolute obligation to pursue the democratic or, for that matter, any other ideal in all circumstances and at all costs. There is no more an obligation to bring about a disaster when insisting on democratic principle than there would be for a craftsman to break a valuable tool by using it in an operation where its breakage can reasonably be foreseen.

NON-ELITES AND DEMOCRACY

From the mid-1970s onward, elites in Western countries too readily attributed increasingly insecure employment, decreasing labor force participation, stagnating wages, and spreading distrust of constituted authority to a stifling of free markets or, alternatively, a failure to offset the harsh workings of markets with adequate welfare and training programs for workers. The 2008–2009 financial crisis and its aftermath challenged both views and made trends among non-elites, especially the increasing insecurity of work, evident. Political consequences included controversial and economically costly bailouts of corporations, banks, and other financial institutions; a splintering of well-established political parties; the Brexit referendum and the startling presidential victory of Donald Trump in 2016; and the spread of stridently populist-nationalist parties and governments. Although not a direct consequence of the crisis, mass migrations to Europe and North America by people fleeing violence, joblessness, disease, shortages of food and water, and dire effects of climate change in many parts of the non-Western world heightened feelings of insecurity among non-elite populations in Western countries. When the United States, United Kingdom, Sweden, and the Netherlands crossed the postindustrial threshold in the late 1940s and early 1950s, bureaucratic and service workers accounted for 40 percent of their workforces (Bell 1973, 123–64; see table 1.1). With lags of ten or twenty years, a similar proportion marked workforces in Austria, Australia, Belgium, Canada, Denmark, France, New Zealand, Norway, Switzerland, West Germany, and the industrialized regions of Greece, Italy, Portugal, and Spain. During the decades that followed, the proportion of bureaucratic and service workers doubled, that of manual industrial workers declined steadily, and numbers of agricultural and artisan workers, many of whom became owners of technologically and organizationally complex farms and businesses, dwindled to single digits.

For many citizens, the initial experience of postindustrialism was an unexpected general affluence resulting from increased levels of real income for families headed by steadily employed, usually male, wage and salary earners. Families in lower occupational and income strata began to find themselves with hours, days, even weeks of leisure, and enough money to get some satisfactions from it. Like rich persons historically, ordinary North Americans, West Europeans, and Antipodeans began to view leisure diversions as important parts of life that for the bulk of them was no longer a matter of ceaseless work.

Starting in the mid-1970s, however, the partial acculturation of non-elites to circumstances loosely resembling those of a leisured class began to fade. As a result of increasing automation and other technological advances, much work became more sophisticated and intellectually demanding. It required substantial training and some comprehension of the technological and interdependent nature of work tasks. The prestige of preferred occupations lessened as the incomes, influence, and conditions of work and leisure they afforded were more approximated by other occupations. The relative affluence enjoyed by less prestigious occupational categories increasingly became somewhat illusory because once families in them obtained middle-class possessions and adopted middle-class lifestyles, they discovered that little surplus income remained.

From the average person's perspective, it was unclear what was happening. Men who had, in the 1950s and 1960s, elected to begin working in a manufacturing plant immediately after completing secondary school, confident that they could do as well as or better than university-bound school mates, began to suffer permanent layoffs. Many of those armed with university degrees and working their way up career ladders of large business corporations began to be victims of downsizing or outsourcing. What these persons could not readily grasp was that many good jobs that had supported a middle-class lifestyle on one income were beginning to disappear.

Unemployment and underemployment, which had been mitigated during the 1950s and 1960s by lengthened periods of education and by millions of jobs in the military and defense industries in response to the Cold War, became more of a problem. Shifts of job opportunities from inner cities to suburbs or to other geographic regions undermined social capital and networks in neighborhoods, leaving large numbers of youth unemployed or underemployed, segregated from adult life, and with lessened hopes for bright futures (Wilson 1997; Putnam 2000, 2015; Packer 2013). In these ways, work insecurities began to pose threats to humane, orderly, and tranquil societies, although the threats did not stem, as during Western history, from the clashing economic interests and political orientations of large agricultural and artisan, manual industrial, and bureaucratic and service components of workforces discussed in chapter 1.

Dramatized by a "misery index" in the United States that combined inflation and unemployment rates to reach 20 percent in 1980, work insecurities were exacerbated by subsequent trends. Technological innovations steadily reduced the need for mental work performed by bureaucratic and service workers. More and more, computers oversaw much routine manual and bureaucratic work that had earlier required human decisions and actions. With increasing frequency, profit-maximizing business executives shifted operations to plants and retail outlets utilizing robots and other automated machines. During the 1990s and after, ever more capacious high-speed computers, the Internet, and an array of mobile devices for instant communication allowed thousands of uses that previously took much time and accounted for much employment. A globalization of labor markets, in which corporations roamed the world in search of cheap labor, aggravated technological trends. The overall effect was to make full-time employment more precarious because there appeared to be few job categories that could not conceivably be eliminated by introducing some automated scheme, thinning an organizational structure, or relocating jobs to cheaper labor markets at home or abroad.

In an important book, *Men Without Work*, economist Nicolas Eberstadt observes that in the United States between the early 1950s and 2016, the participation of working-age men in the officially defined labor force dropped by 18 percentage points and the proportion of men aged twenty and older without paid work more than doubled from 14 percent to about 32 percent (2016, 20). During 2015 on a monthly average, 22 percent of American men between the ages of twenty and sixty-five had no paying job of any kind, and in a condition of "near-full employment" during 2016, one of every six men in the historically prime working ages of twenty-five to fifty-four had no paying job, which was down from one in sixteen during the 1980s (22). Other research, reported in 2017, found that since the 2008–2009 financial crisis 1.5 million prime working-age Americans simply "vanished" from the workforce, with many falling into drug addiction and poverty (Casselman 2017).

Insecure employment was further underscored by a projection that in 2020 freelance and temporary workers, day laborers, contract workers, and others performing "on-demand" and "gig economy" jobs would comprise 40 percent of the officially defined U.S. labor force (MBO Partners 2015). In Europe, around a third of the continent's labor force were in "alternative employment arrangements" without the level of benefits for health care, retirement, and unemployment that full-time, regular employment usually ensured (Brighton et al. 2015).

For many years, elites and observers paid little attention to these trends, principally because women were entering workforces in large numbers. However, the entrance of women slowed in the late 1990s and employed women began to drop or be pushed out of workforces. Between 2001 and 2016, for example, a half million jobs in the U.S. retail sector, many of them held by women, were eliminated. In terms of working-age male participation in its workforce, by 2015 the United States ranked twenty-second among the OECD's twenty-three original member countries; only Italy ranked lower (Eberstadt 2016, 51). Between February 2020 and February 2021, the Coronavirus pandemic made ten million Americans, half of them women, unemployed. Although the official unemployment rate in February 2021 was 6.3 percent, it took no account of the massively shrunken workforce and was around 10 percent. Worse, the pandemic transformed much work by forcing additional automation and digitalization as consumers become accustomed to working and shopping online. This erased large numbers of low-wage food service, retail, hospitality, customer service, and office support jobs that accounted, prepandemic, for one in four jobs in the United States (Tyson and Lund 2021).

These workforce changes suggest that many North Americans and Europeans have lost or are losing the ability to claim incomes and social statuses on grounds that their work is necessary to economic and societal functioning. It is not that work, especially highly educated and technologically sophisticated work, is dispensable in the production and distribution functions of Western economies. Rather, given the rapid proliferation of goods and services involving automated or virtual processes, greatly accelerated by the pandemic, the need for work serves poorly to justify any person's claim to a job and the social status associated with it, unless he or she possesses some skill or knowledge that happens to be in short supply.

As an overall consequence of these many changes, *demoralization*—the loss of individual morale and loss of respect for established social norms—has become widespread among working- and middle-class non-elites and, more dramatically and often violently, among growing underclasses, many of whose members are, strictly speaking, surplus to postindustrial needs for labor. "Diseases of despair"—alcoholism, narcotics addiction, opioids, and suicides—manifest this demoralization (Case and Deacon 2020) as do millenarian beliefs and movements, such as the QAnon belief that the world is run by a satanic group of elite pedophiles against whom

Donald Trump waged a top-secret mission to bring the evildoers to justice.

In his study of the havoc wrought by millenarian movements when the feudal order was breaking up in medieval Europe, Norman Cohn concluded in his book *The Pursuit of the Millennium* that millenarianism stemmed from "the amorphous mass of people . . . who could find no assured and recognized place in society" and who formed "a restlessly and utterly ruthless group [that] recognized no claims save that of its own supposed mission" (1961, 282, 285). As British political theorist John Gray has observed, the classic millenarian syndrome is a belief in vast conspiracies and the workings of dark forces (2007, 25). The proliferation of fanatical movements such as QAnon, which attracts several million people, is an ominous sign of non-elite insecurity and demoralization.

THE POPULIST THREAT TO DEMOCRACY

Throughout the twentieth century's second half, intellectuals and political leaders exemplified by Margaret Thatcher and Ronald Reagan were preoccupied with ways in which economic experience discredited various collectivist doctrines that appealed to many humane and sympathetic people in earlier times (Fukuyama 2012). It became undeniable, not only under state socialism in the Soviet Union and Eastern Europe but more widely in Latin America, Southeast and South Asia, that in basic matters of production—whether agricultural and artisan, manual industrial, or bureaucratic and service—efficient economic performance depends on making substantial appeals to the individual self-interests of owners, managers, and workers.

This made examining the increasingly widespread insecurity of work awkward because doing so could easily invite charges of hostility to an economic system, capitalism, that appeared to be incomparably more productive than any other. Capitalism's apparent superiority over socialism expanded the ranks and prestige of principled capitalists who championed free markets as the solution for most problems. Faith in free markets, privatization, low taxes, and as little government regulation as possible had always been strong among American, British, French, German, and other Western elites. From the 1980s onward, however, it acquired a new intensity with the ascendance of neoliberals in political and business arenas and their partial ascendance in media and intellectual circles. Subjecting declining postindustrial needs for work and the increasing insecurity of much work to scrutiny was decidedly out of favor.

At the twenty-first century's start, a general conclusion that Keynesian economic policies lead eventually to serious inflation removed much of the enthusiasm for sharply modifying the life chances of people through open-ended welfare state programs and measures. A widespread revulsion against the government bureaucracies required to administer the welfare state's redistributive and regulatory policies also undermined that enthusiasm. However, the lengthy economic recession that began in 2008–2009 and the Coronavirus pandemic's economic ravages ten years later ended whatever enthusiasm remained for strict economic liberalization. Central banks—notably the U.S. Federal Reserve under Ben Bernanke and the European Central Bank under Mario Draghi—made large-scale purchases of government bonds and other financial assets to inject money that was essentially created out of thin air into crippled economies. To combat the pandemic, Western governments spent huge sums of borrowed money to spur economic recovery and protect public health. The pandemic accelerated the trend to worry less about government deficits and national debt and more about insufficiently activist governments. Neoliberal demands for deregulation, low taxes, limited domestic spending, and free markets could not cope with the pandemic's magnitude and dreadful effects, and those demands effectively vanished.

The insecure character of much work in advanced postindustrial conditions has spread steadily in nearly all Western countries for fifty years, and it has been impervious to neoliberal and welfare state panaceas. Many of the several millions of working-age men outside Western labor forces and the formerly employed women who joined them before the pandemic struck in 2020 as well as a sizable proportion of the tens of millions made unemployed by the pandemic can probably not be reabsorbed into Western workforces. Of course, some of these persons do not want to be reabsorbed even if it were possible. Some prefer idleness, some have disabilities, some have been able to retire early and comfortably, many lack skills or mindsets required for available jobs, and others view available jobs as too poorly paid or too unpleasant to perform. Yet there is little doubt that clear and pressing needs for many kinds of jobs and workers diminish.

Instead of recognizing and grappling with this long-term problem, populist-nationalist leaders, like Donald Trump in the United States; Boris Johnson and Nigel Farage in the United Kingdom; Geert Wilders, founder of the Party of Freedom in the Netherlands; Marine Le Pen at the head of National Rally in France; Jimmie Akesson, the Sweden Democrats leader; Albert Rösti, leader of the Swiss People's Party; Matteo Salvini, leader of The League in Italy; Santiago Abascal and Spain's Vox Party; and Viktor Orbán and Jaroslaw Kacyzinski, who at present respectively control the Hungarian and Polish governments, exploit non-elite resentments that stem primarily from work insecurity. They promise to displace the allegedly nefarious elites and political establishments they hold responsible for this insecurity. In service to self-aggrandizement and political gain, they violate codes of elite trust and collaboration and deliberately bring non-elite anxieties to a boil while proclaiming that they alone can allay them. Because they ignore the intractability of work insecurity in advanced postindustrial conditions, their pronouncements are at best games of "bait and switch" and at worst body blows to democratic institutions and processes.

Despite populism's rapid spread and the swift rise of populist-nationalist leaders to power, explanations adhere prevailingly to a gradualist, non-elite perspective. In *Cultural Backlash: Trump, Brexit, and Authoritarian Populism*, Pippa Norris and Ronald Inglehart (2019) emphasize broad changes among non-elites to explain "authoritarian populism," which they define as "a style of rhetoric claiming that legitimate power rests with 'the people' not the elites" (2019, 4; see also Müller 2016; Mounk 2018). They posit non-elite cultural backlashes as the main cause of authoritarian populism and argue that backlashes are a consequence of the improved living conditions and individual security that created a "silent revolution" in values during the 1960s and 1970s. The "revolution" eventually generated conservative and authoritarian reactions, mainly among older voters (2019, 14–15). The argument is nuanced and supported by survey data on public opinion and voting patterns underpinning more than fifty authoritarian populist parties, most of them in Western democracies. Not oblivious to the importance of idiosyncratic populist leaders like Donald Trump, Boris Johnson, Marine Le Pen, or Nigel Farage or to contingent events in each country examined, Norris and Inglehart contend that, as a phenomenon, authoritarian populism "is much broader than any individual and thus requires a more general theory" (2019, 13).

Cas Mudde, a respected student of European politics, portrays contemporary populism as a new political-ideological current and attributes it to several structural changes and their political effects, most especially policy failures of liberal democracies in conditions of "liberal globalization" (2004, 2018; Mudde and Kaltwasser 2017). More specifically, Mudde argues that growing economic inequalities and cognitive political mobilizations centered on them have created dissatisfied European populations. In addition, a broad elite consensus about neoliberal economic policies and the desirability of supranational undertakings, such as the European Union and the International Monetary Fund, has lessened the effectiveness of mainstream political parties and made them more similar, while a radically transformed media landscape has provided populist leaders with publicity and unprecedented access to mass publics. Like Norris and Inglehart's cultural backlash thesis, Mudde's analysis is complex, and he does not ignore the importance of canny populist leaders who benefit from improved organization and propaganda.

Francis Fukuyama (2014) portrays populism as a type of regime pursuing popular but unsustainable policies. It adheres to a legitimation principle that anchors political power in the wills of ordinary people located in ethnonational or quasi-class constellations and induces a personalistic and responsive leadership style. Fukuyama ascribes recent populist surges to economic, political, and cultural circumstances and trends that have produced institutional decay, especially the lessening of legal constraints. To these broad causes, Fukuyama adds liberal policy failures that have deflated incomes and social statuses among working and lower middle strata and triggered a "politics of resentment" that creates gridlocked and ineffective governments ("vetocracies") together with racial, ethnic, and religious identity fears among native-born populations in the face of swelling immigration. In Fukuyama's view, populism feeds on and accelerates institutional decay by assaulting independent judiciaries, centralizing executive power, engaging in nepotism, and hollowing out electoral processes through increasing manipulation of voter opinions. He treats populism as a key beneficiary and perpetrator of institutional decay and, thus, the deterioration of liberal democracy. His analysis is also more complex than a summary conveys.

Explanations of contemporary populism that center on non-elites are not wrong, but more attention should be given to elite and leadership agency. What explanations emphasizing the conditions and attitudes of non-elites fail to consider is that, once they acquire significant amounts of prominence and power, populist leaders deliberately exacerbate the societal divisions and grievances that underlay their rise. To a considerable extent, they act *autogenously*, that is, independently of non-elite influence or aid.

Donald J. Trump was (and remains) a quintessentially autogenic populist leader. His behavior and actions as U.S. president have been cataloged and assessed in scores of books and thousands of media accounts (see especially Woodward 2018; Rucker and Leonnig 2020). Occupying the White House for four years, despite a complete lack of experience in national-level politics and policymaking, Trump behaved as a "pluto-populist," bragging about his personal wealth and lavish lifestyle while persuading millions of followers to support policies and actions that mainly served the wealthy. His endlessly repeated vow to "Make America Great Again!" was a subterfuge that left plutocratic wealth and power unmentioned and untouched. A pied piper, Trump tweeted daily, even hourly, to followers, glorifying what he claimed to be accomplishing and impugning critics. He delighted being the star at rallies, delivering rambling speeches in which he told audiences their problems were the fault of his foes: "incompetent" predecessors, "disgraceful" opponents in Congress, and a "deep state" of government officials trying to subvert him. Journalists who contested Trump's tweets and speeches as factually false were claimed to be contemptible traffickers in "fake news." In classic piper mode, Trump shouted to one large audience at a rally during 2018, "Ah, the elite, the elite! Did you ever see the elite? [loud boos] YOU ARE THE ELITE!"

Trump's presidency was markedly personalistic and nepotistic. Family members held the highest White House advisory and campaign positions. One after another in televised cabinet meetings, secretaries were made to praise Trump. White House staff feared his ire, and staff turnover was twice that of any modern presidency. He expanded the executive branch's power and invoked "national security" to justify executive orders having little or nothing to do with foreign policy, military, or intelligence matters. Republicans in Congress were supine defenders of Trump, with those in the Senate routinely ignoring legislation passed by the House after Democrats gained control of it in 2018 and collaborating with Trump's effort to remake the federal judiciary by confirming some two hundred conservative court nominees with almost no scrutiny.

In politics, Trump made no serious effort to attract voters beyond the minority who voted for him in 2016. With a 40 to 45 percent job approval rating, instead of trying to unite the polity, he enflamed its rural-urban, racial, ethnoreligious, and gender divisions. He regularly violated norms of restrained partisanship by attacking opponents as "losers" if not criminals who should be in jail. Trump's arbitrary actions as president were without precedent in American political history, and his continuing refusal to accept the legitimacy of the 2020 presidential election, in which Joseph R. Biden Jr. won seven million more votes than Trump, constitutes a clear threat to American democracy.

A dramatic manifestation of this threat was Trump's incitement of several thousand fervent followers, some of whom had weapons, to march to the Capitol building in Washington, DC, on January 6, 2021, and prevent Congress, which was meeting in joint session, from certifying the presidential election of Joseph R. Biden Jr. Overrunning the Capitol police, Trump supporters, some waving QAnon banners, swarmed through the building in search of allegedly perfidious members of Congress as well as Vice President Michael Pence, who was presiding at the joint certifying session. Five persons died, two later committed suicide, and 140 police officers were injured. For several hours, Trump, sitting safely in the White House a mile away, did nothing to stop the assault, and it was not until late afternoon that his supporters were driven from the Capitol by force. Subsequent investigations and arrests of several hundred of the assailants revealed that more than half of those arrested were persons variously experiencing personal bankruptcies, home evictions, indebtedness, and unpaid taxes (Frankel 2021). They personified insecure non-elites and people seized by millenarian beliefs.

Boris Johnson, the British populist-nationalist leader most responsible for the narrow Brexit vote in June 2016 and the British leader most liked by Donald Trump, was elected leader of the Conservative Party by party members in July 2019, and the Conservatives' working majority in Parliament thereupon made Johnson prime minister. Preceding the Brexit referendum, Johnson likened European Union efforts to unite Europe to those of Hitler and Napoleon, engaged in Islamophobia and spread the specter of millions of Muslims entering Britain via the European Union, lied that 350,000 pounds sterling per week would be recouped for the National Health Service by leaving the European Union and asserted that leaving would be a simple matter of "taking back control" and restoring Britain's greatness. Johnson's populist-nationalist demagogy was peddled by a faction in the Conservative Party, tabloid newspapers, and Donald Trump's other favorite British political figure, Nigel Farage, then leader of the U.K. Independence Party and later of the Brexit Party.

Installed in No. 10 Downing Street, Johnson has dominated the political scene to a greater extent than any recent Conservative prime minister. Displaying little regard for policy complexities and customary niceties of politics, he vowed to steamroll Brexit through the House of Commons with or without an E.U. exit "deal." Not having a firm Conservative majority in the House constrained Johnson somewhat, as did the dislike and distrust that many senior Conservative leaders had for him, not to mention the disdain of Labour and Liberal party leaders. Like Trump, Johnson is a populist-nationalist leader inclined to wield executive power autogenously in ways that trespass upon constitutional norms and accepted political practices.

In a secret speech to activists in his *Fidesz* (Federation of Young Democrats) Party prior to Hungary's parliamentary election in 2010, Viktor Orbán said that his goal was to build a "central field of force." The Fidesz election victory that year and the party's subsequent victories in 2015 and 2019 elections enabled Orbán to realize his goal. Outsized Fidesz majorities in the electorally skewed parliament, a centralization of executive power and weakened constitutional protections, the muzzling of media and educational institutions along with curtailed civic and property rights gave Orbán control of the entire Hungarian state (Lengyel and Ilonzski 2016). Systematic clientelism extended his control to the economy. As prime minister, Orbán has stirred public anxieties and fears, demonized migrants, and attacked critics, notably the expatriate Hungarian George Soros, depicted by Orbán as Hungary's mortal enemy. Although Orbán has been solidly entrenched, indications of corruption have increased, economic growth has slowed, public and private debts to foreign lenders have swelled, and Hungary has been shunned by E.U. governments other than Poland's. Although Orbán radiates confidence and high self-esteem, his political adversaries are increasingly united, and he must deal with disobedient business oligarchs who have significant influence and autonomy. During 2020–2021, the Coronavirus pandemic's savage impact make it uncertain if Orbán will sustain his political dominance.

Following the Peace and Justice Party's victory in Poland's 2015 parliamentary elections, a highly centralized and semi-formal structure of power was erected, with Jaroslaw Kaczynski, the party's chairman, at its center (Pakulski 2016). Top state officials were replaced by party loyalists, state media were renamed "national media," and reforms of the education system implanted Polish and Christian values in schools. A decommunized "Fourth Republic" was proclaimed, Polish history was reinterpreted in martyrologic anti-Russian and anti-German terms, and Lech Walesa, the leader of Solidarity, was accused of having been a communist secret police agent. The Minister of Defense duly delivered a dubious report alleging that an on-board explosion, not bad weather, caused the Smolensk airplane crash that killed Lech Kaczynski, Jaroslaw's twin brother, and his elite entourage in 2010. The military high command was purged, and a Civil Defense force, suspected of being a Peace and Justice militia, was organized. The Constitutional Tribunal and the Supreme Court were incapacitated and stacked with compliant jurists. Poland became the first E.U. member state to be investigated and condemned for breaching E.U. laws, the first to be threatened by E.U. Article 7 sanctions, and the first to be condemned for undermining judicial independence. However, external setbacks did not diminish electoral support for Kaczynski's leadership, which was boosted by regular welfare "handouts" and the powerful Catholic Church's open support. As with Orbán in Hungary, the Coronavirus pandemic's devastating impact on public health and the economy makes the political prospects of Kaczynski and his Peace and Justice Party uncertain.

CONCLUSIONS

Populist-nationalist leaders such as Trump, Johnson, Orbán, and Kaczynski have been the most prominent advocates of major social and political changes in Western societies. Regarding themselves as located outside the bureaucratic structures of their societies, as bitter foes of those structures, and as performing a vital teaching or corrective function in matters of public sentiment, these and other populist leaders are inclined toward a general notion of equality as the normative standard against which political actions and outcomes should be judged. They profess to believe that a society characterized by a rough equality is possible and that most persons will ultimately agree about its worth. In these beliefs, populists are residual bearers of the utopianism that figured so prominently in Western political thought during modern history.

A caveat about politics is that elites and other influential political actors have an interest in managing and limiting conflicts in a society only if they enjoy considerable safety and security in their own political and social statuses. When unsafe and insecure, elites and other political actors must devote their thought and energies to repressing or annihilating enemies. This means that conflicts can be managed and contained by elites and other influential actors only if major reversals of status, such as populists promise and threaten, do not impend. The absence of such status reversals during the modern histories of the Anglo-American, Scandinavian, and Low Countries and the comparatively effective elite management of conflicts in them over long periods illustrate the caveat.

Is this to say that, despite what populist leaders claim, most Westerners already live in the best possible world? Of course not. Reforms of extant political institutions and practices will always be required. Because of technological and social change, arrangements that worked under previous conditions must constantly be adjusted to work under new ones. In the postindustrial societies of today and tomorrow, populist leaders and rulers cannot abolish discontent, envy, and conflict because these societies inescapably involve unequal chances for individuals to achieve and enjoy statuses to which all or most aspire but only some can achieve.

Chapter Four

Ultimate and Instrumental Values in Liberal Democracy

As developed originally by well-off bourgeois strata during the eighteenth and nineteenth centuries, especially in English-speaking countries and northwestern Europe, liberalism emphasized freedom from arbitrary political and legal restraints and from political interference in legitimately private activities. Combining beliefs in religious tolerance, freedom of speech for those who discussed issues responsibly, and the social utility and inherent fairness of freedom for economic entrepreneurs, liberalism did not originally have any clear egalitarian thrust.

During the nineteenth century, the countries in which this liberal doctrine was widely accepted achieved dominance over much of the world. Consequently, large parts of their populations experienced great increases in prosperity, leisure, and self-confidence. With that, many adherents of liberalism in dominant Western countries found that political order and social peace were compatible with, and even facilitated by, wider and wider extensions of the suffrage. They discovered, in other words, that steady increases in national power and prosperity and the multiplication of attractive and reasonably influential job opportunities permitted the formal democratization of their governments without opening the way to participation by any great number of illiberal and deeply discontented persons. Thus, the English-speaking countries, the Low Countries, and the Scandinavian countries enjoyed obvious success in democratizing their governments and in extending liberal practices. Most other West European countries moved in the same direction, although more severe conflicts within their elites and societies made success less complete.

In this way, evolution toward stable liberal democracies gradually came to be seen as a plausible, even a natural progression. Liberals became increasingly committed to egalitarian values in terms of individual rights, including the right of suffrage. During the twentieth century, this evolution led to the assumption that all the principal features of modern liberal democracies were equal components of ultimate liberal values. These features included (1) constitutional government, as distinguished from powerful monarchies and from the military and other dictatorships that occur sporadically in unstable political regimes; (2) political, administrative, and judicial practices that strongly respect personal dignity by requiring that governments follow preestablished laws, that they put themselves at a substantial disadvantage in proving persons to be wrongdoers, and that they refrain from governing at all in certain more or less understood matters, such as religion and other forms of belief; and (3) democracy, at least in the sense of universal suffrage exercised in real electoral contests that determine leading government personnel.

The liberal became a staunch democrat, and the general pattern of government in the liberal societies of the West came to be termed "liberal democratic." However, while this evolution of liberalism into liberal democracy was natural enough in the economic, global, and political contexts of Western countries, in most other countries the twin commitments to liberal and democratic values are frequently, perhaps always, in conflict. This is because opening effective political participation to all organized factions in free and fair electoral contests leads inevitably to political claims that are unacceptable to many entrenched interests. Such interests are commonly numerous enough and well enough situated to carry out coups or electoral frauds that sweep away threats to their ways of life and privileges. In either respect, attempts to achieve liberal democracy merely by instituting democratic suffrage and holding elections are almost certain to be unsuccessful. This was amply demonstrated by the repeated military coups that terminated newly established democratic regimes in Latin America during the 150 years that followed independence from Spanish and Portuguese rule. The general pattern of political struggles has been the same in Africa, the Middle East, and most of South and Southeast Asia since overt colonial rule ended during the decades that followed World War II.

The linking of egalitarian goals such as democracy with liberal goals such as personal freedom and orderly government has involved considerable confusion. It has diverted attention from the elite practices that are everywhere a precondition for liberal democracy, and in doing so it has been harmful to the liberal cause. A more sophisticated understanding would see nearly all the features of democracy as *instrumental* liberal values, which in certain elite conditions may provide or promote *ultimate* liberal values. Constitutional government and at least some version of governmental practice respectful of personal dignity are empirically necessary to a liberal regime. But democracy in the sense of an extended or universal suffrage is not strictly necessary for such a regime, and in many ordinary political circumstances may be inimical to it.

To suppose that a liberal should ultimately prefer democratic government for its own sake is, in fact, a somewhat naïve and provincial position. It is a position that is speciously plausible to well-off persons who happen to live under stable liberal regimes and whose favored circumstances enable them to derive personal satisfactions from democratic participation in their own government. But it has little plausibility for those who live under illiberal regimes or for less well-off and less self-confident persons in liberal states. In general, such persons have no interest in diligent, part-time excursions into the kind of limited and negotiated politics that offer considerable satisfactions to educated and relatively privileged citizens. Similarly, in contemplating liberal safeguards against violations of personal dignity, less well-off and less self-confident and secure persons often conclude that these safeguards do less to protect their own dignity, which they may feel they have little of anyway, than they prevent effective control of interests they fear or for which they have no serious sympathy.

For liberal doctrine to obtain the allegiance of larger circles than the limited number of well-off amateur politicians who like democratic politics for the satisfactions it affords them, it is necessary to find an *ultimate* liberal value that can be more widely shared. At the same time, this value must be distinguished carefully from *instrumental* liberal values that may or may not contribute empirically to its realization.

THE ULTIMATE LIBERAL VALUE

A social milieu of "free people" is the ultimate liberal value. This is a milieu in which people deal with each other as equals and in which no one claims for her- or himself, nor expects to accord to others, systematically greater deference or higher privilege. The historical contexts that the expression "free people" calls to mind are those that liberals envisage as ideal: the Switzerland of William Tell, the Holland of William the Silent, the America of George Washington. However, to evoke those contexts is to make it clear that liberals value equality only insofar as it is linked to an active and individualistic freedom. The liberal cares nothing for, and even abhors, the kind of equality that might prevail in a community of unassertive persons wholly submissive to custom or prevailing opinion.

The ultimate liberal value is thus a social milieu in which persons are free and equal in active social and political roles. Institutionalized politics and government practices that prevent violations of personal dignity contribute *instrumentally* toward achieving this. Unstable politics involving coups and court intrigues as well as government practices that readily degrade people contribute *instrumentally* toward preventing or destroying it. As for democracy, or universal suffrage, its effectiveness as an *instrumental device*—in Joseph Schumpeter's term a "method" (1942, 269)—for achieving the desired liberal milieu varies with circumstances.

Characterizing a social milieu of free people as the ultimate liberal value implies that liberal attitudes normally require a substantial degree of good fortune, self-confidence, and optimism about the future. This is because the opportunity to interact with other persons freely and equally is of little value to those who do not possess the kinds of occupational and social roles and resulting temperaments that facilitate such interaction. Without changes in their situations, persons whose roles are seriously degrading, punishing, frightful, or merely boring cannot be influenced toward, or converted to, liberal attitudes. Liberal attitudes can never be contagious except among people already disposed by a certain amount of good fortune to accept them. In any complex and bureaucratically organized society, there is always a shortage of the kinds of roles that enable people to interact freely, vigorously, and equally with each other. This means that pursuit of the ultimate liberal goal may sometimes mean "giving to him that hath" and "from him that hath not take away even that which he hath." Less abstrusely, and as an example, any commitment to "social justice" that involves, as a matter of overriding principle, concessions to, or privileges for, persons and groups in recompense for their past misfortunes is incompatible with a sophisticated allegiance to the ultimate liberal goal. When granted on a principled and wide basis, such special concessions and privileges threaten to undermine the advantaged positions of those who are already liberal. In so doing, they help to undermine or destroy liberal attitudes where they exist without providing any certainty that those being helped will themselves adopt such attitudes. No informed liberal can favor such schemes on a principled basis.

ELITISM

Distinguishing between the ultimate liberal value and instrumental liberal values places democracy and other egalitarian measures on a different footing from what most recent Western political thought has presumed. The distinction reemphasizes Schumpeter's conception of democracy as a political method that depends for its workings on several propitious and underlying circumstances. If liberals prefer ultimately to associate actively with free persons on a basis of equality, then, obviously, an entire society of "free persons" that is governed democratically and is otherwise egalitarian is the liberal *ideal.* Liberals would greatly prefer this to an oligarchic society in which only a small number of privileged people interact on a free and equal basis.

Yet historical contingencies that produced societies at once liberal and egalitarian have been extremely rare. They have mostly been tiny communities located in agrarian and isolated parts of Western territories that were advantaged over the rest of the world by early technological progress. Any liberal reasonably familiar with history would not believe that a society that is at once liberal and egalitarian is attainable in most circumstances. A society that is considerably more stratified but that nevertheless has an upper layer of actively free and equal persons—by no means a common historical situation either—is the most that a liberal can normally hope to attain or preserve.

These considerations point toward *elitism*. Although the liberal's ideal is individualistic participation in a society of equal persons, is she or he honestly an egalitarian? An egalitarian is presumably a person committed to the equalization of people as an ultimate good. When this egalitarian preference is held unconditionally, it is likely to prove incompatible with the liberal's preference for a milieu of free persons within which one can interact as an active equal. It is simply a matter of historical fact that liberals have sometimes enjoyed limited approximations of their ideal that would most probably have been upset or destroyed by thoroughly egalitarian measures.

In eighteenth-century England, for instance, a considerable number of well-off persons enjoyed an approximation of a liberal society in their own interactions. But most of the population was poor, uneducated, disenfranchised, and subject to abusive treatment by authorities when speaking or acting in ways that threatened the well off. It can hardly be supposed that in that time and place the liberal practices that existed among the few would have survived if some force had decreed formal equality for all and then actually implemented the decree by equivalents of today's affirmative action measures and confidence-building exercises for the disadvantaged. Likewise, there can be little doubt that liberal practices in Western societies today would be imperiled if someone established a genuine world government with a full range of taxation and police powers and arrangements designed to ensure that all non-Western countries exercise proportionate shares of influence in the world government's policymaking.

The implication is that a person of liberal persuasion is prudently willing to accept his or her goal in the form of half a loaf if the alternative appears to be no bread at all. In other words, the liberal cannot honestly claim to be a committed egalitarian in the way that some persons are or believe themselves to be. The liberal is willing to live in a society where liberal practice extends only to that part of the population to which her or his associates belong if further equalization can only be attained by upsetting this liberal milieu.

Similarly, the liberal is willing to live in an unequal society that enjoys considerable advantages in technology and access to world resources if (1) international equalization is not attainable without drastically curtailing living standards in the advantaged society, so that its liberal practices would probably be destroyed, and (2) because of the population ratios involved, there is little prospect that international equalization would create liberal practices in countries whose living standards would only be minutely increased thereby.

To state it forthrightly, the liberal is selfish, although not necessarily more selfish than the average person. The liberal is necessarily *elitist*, however much this may clash with what she or he would prefer as an ideal if ideals could be made real. The liberal has had, or expects to have, enough good fortune to want and value the equal interaction of free and actively individualistic persons. He or she is more self-confident, more self-reliant, and less fearful of powerful persons and interests than the average person historically or at present. The liberal is not, however, committed to inequality. She or he is not among those who prefer a society of unequal and mostly un-free persons in principle.

From the liberal's standpoint, in short, the more socially or geographically extended that a milieu of free and equal people is, the better. But there is no simple, straightforward way to create or extend a society of free and equal persons by political or legal means. It is obvious that, as socialists have argued, one cannot make unequal persons equal merely by declaring them equally qualified to vote and participate in formal politics, as in a democracy. It is also obvious that one cannot make unequal persons equal by enforcing a variety of rules, principles, and standards designed to prevent people from taking advantage of inequality. State socialism tried to do this and failed. The liberal does not seek social advantages as a goal but instead accepts advantages when they afford free and equal interaction with other persons and there are no practical possibilities for widening the circle of liberal persons.

When contemplating political possibilities, the liberal is elitist as regards the desirability and feasibility of democratic practices. But the failure to distinguish the ultimate liberal value from instrumental democratic considerations has caused liberals to misunderstand the real relation of democracy to liberal aims. By treating democratic government as an indistinguishable part of a cluster of goals, liberals have committed the error of thinking that formal equality in political statuses—democracy—is a reliable means for promoting liberal practices. Considered on its own merits, this proposition that universal suffrage, frequent voting, and other democratic measures reliably, that is, regardless of circumstances, promote the interaction of free and actively equal persons should be patently incredible to persons with much political experience or knowledge.

It is more nearly the other way around. Especially among elites, liberal practices such as avoiding the use of political means to pursue drastic social changes are essential to the year-in, year-out acceptance by different factions in a competition for votes that determines who shall hold office and who shall define policies. A "live and let live" disposition among elites, which means a tacit agreement not to exacerbate potentially explosive conflicts and respect each other's vital interests, is the *sine qua non* for any practical and durable degree of democratic politics.

By contrast, in a society whose elites and other influential elements are not liberal, those in political office at any given moment fall into one of two categories. Most commonly, they represent advantaged social strata that do not feel themselves secure against future contingencies. Consequently, they use political power, if they can, to further entrench themselves and those they represent by reducing the freedom of less fortunate strata to upset the existing social and political order. Certainly, notions about political freedom do not restrain them from doing this; they tolerate democratic practices only when it is convenient to do so, and ordinarily that is not for very long.

The other, less common category of political office holders in a society where liberal practices are not firmly established consists of those who have been victorious in a recent revolutionary upheaval. Normally, these persons hold egalitarian convictions. But they are aware, as modern liberals are not, that the newly triumphant political elite must act in the way just described. Certainly, while its members may regard "government by the people" as consistent with their convictions, they have no intention of letting the opportunity to reform society in an egalitarian direction slip through their hands. They will not take the chance of setting up an electoral competition that might be won by persons not sharing their convictions. Instead, they will feel obliged to keep the electoral process effectively controlled to produce results that they alone approve of so long as they are able to do so. In short, triumphant revolutionary leaders will ignore the democratic practices that are of interest to liberals.

PROSPECTS

Has the liberal's conflation of ultimate and instrumental values lasted too long to be reparable? Possibly it has. Since at least World War II, almost everyone who might be considered a liberal has characterized the ultimate liberal goal in democratic terms. The unanimity and fervor with which persons regarding themselves as liberals have urged extensive democratization of their own societies and of illiberal non-Western societies indicate a near-total confusion of cause and effect in their understanding of political possibilities. This confusion has greatly weakened the self-recognition of liberals to a remarkable degree.

It is uncertain whether liberal-minded elites in Western countries are any longer capable of identifying and taking the kinds of initiatives that might deal constructively with the world's problems. Their members are blind to the fact that in their own societies the spread of democratic suffrage in ways that did not fundamentally undermine liberal practices depended on the prior existence of a consensual unified elite. It also probably depended on the West's substantial world economic and military dominance. Consequently, members of liberal-minded elites cannot comprehend that the absence of these conditions in most non-Western countries may necessitate less than democratic means of governing them. Until in some way elites in such illiberal countries become consensually or at least imperfectly unified, attempts to install liberal democracy in them are bound to fail.

I have tried to show how liberal democracy can be put on a firmer intellectual and comparative footing than recent political thought has recognized. Writing as a liberal, Joseph Schumpeter correctly saw that democracy is a method, or in my usage an *instrumental value*, that in appropriate elite conditions can serve the ultimate liberal value of a free people. Addressing English-speaking readers in the early 1940s, whom he plausibly assumed to be of liberal persuasion, Schumpeter did not highlight the historical distinctiveness, indeed the rarity, of the competitive democracy he described. Nor, perhaps conscious of his American location (at Harvard University when he wrote) and of America's egalitarian proclivities, did Schumpeter think it prudent to highlight the elitism implicit in his description of democracy.

Numerous, mainly American critics of Schumpeter did this soon enough. Labeling his theory "democratic elitism," they portrayed it as an unwanted, even outrageous closure of the open-ended road to ideal democracy that they regarded their society and, they wanted to believe, all societies are traveling (for example, Bachrach 1967; see also Sartori 1987, 152–63; Best and Higley 2010). Critics of Schumpeter hope to find some less elite-centered and more impersonal and universal form of democracy. This is probably a forlorn hope. They must come to terms with realistic limits to what is possible in politics. When they do, their understanding of democracy will not differ much from what Schumpeter understood.

Chapter Five

The Arab Spring Folly

A central contention in chapter 1 is that disunified elites and unstable, often autocratic regimes constitute the modal pattern of politics in modern history and today. In most places and times, politics are plagued by sharp and unremitting conflicts between warring elites, each faction seeking political supremacy without much regard for costs or rules. Ruthless power plays are routine, and the lives of elite persons are full of risk. Mistrusting each other and knowing that a misstep could be fatal, elite persons and factions typically regard democratic elections as another way enemies will undermine them. Attempts to install democracy, or an incipient degree of it, give rise to crises that trigger coups or other political usurpations.

A principal contention in chapter 3 is that consensual unified elites are stable democracy's *sine qua non*. This clashes with the teleological assumption that democracy is a natural condition that would exist everywhere if the Augean political stable were cleansed of nefarious elites and regimes. It also clashes with the common assumption that it is non-elites, not elites, who create and sustain democracy. The Arab Spring in 2011 and its aftermaths demonstrated the folly of both assumptions. Getting rid of perceptibly nefarious elites and regimes merely enabled other persons and groups to seize and consolidate government power with little regard for democratic niceties, while non-elite mobilizations to "choose democracy" led to deep divisions that made stable democracy most unlikely.

This chapter examines efforts to bring about the downfalls of ruling elites and autocratic regimes to create democracy in Libya, Syria, Tunisia, and Egypt during and since 2011 as well as earlier and lengthier efforts to do this in Afghanistan and Iraq. I hasten to disclaim specialist knowledge of the six countries; I am only a general observer of their politics. My knowledge is deepened, however, by an authoritative account of futile efforts by the United States and its European allies to create democracy by effecting elite and regime change in Iraq, Afghanistan, Libya, Syria, and Egypt: Philip H. Gordon's *Losing the Long Game: The False Promise of Regime Change in the Middle East* (2020). His account concretizes several generalizations about politics in this book's preceding chapters. Gordon was a senior figure in the U.S. national security and diplomatic elite during much of the period. Writing from a Washington perspective, he shows that removing or attempting to remove autocratic elites and regimes was hardly conducive to democracy. Although Gordon mentions Tunisia only in passing, its tentative democratization will be examined more closely here.

IRAQ AND AFGHANISTAN

The military invasion of Iraq by the United States in March 2003 was the most dramatic instance of liquidating an autocratic ruler and regime to clear the way for democracy. Although creating democracy was not the only reason for the invasion, most American political and military leaders believed that if the Saddam Hussein elite and Ba'athist regime were eradicated, "the first Arab democracy" would result (Ricks 2006, 150–65; Gordon 2020, 127). Accordingly, on May 16, 2003, Order No. 1 of the U.S.-installed Coalition Provisional Authority (CPA) in Baghdad dictated the "De-Ba'athification of Iraq Society" by purging as many as 85,000 Ba'ath Party members from their positions. A week later, CPA Order No. 2, "Dissolution of Iraqi Entities," disbanded the armed forces (385,000 men), Interior Ministry (285,000 men), and presidential security units (50,000 men). Order No. 2 further declared that "any person holding the rank under the former regime of Colonel or above, or its equivalent, will be deemed a Senior Party Member to be fired from his position, made ineligible for a pension, and banned from future employment in the public sector" (Ricks 2006, 158–59; Gordon 2020, 128–29). The two edicts consigned thousands of influential Iraqis—industrial managers, government administrators and mid-level functionaries, professors, and schoolteachers, not to mention military and police officers—to the economic scrap heap, along with family members dependent on them. U.S. intelligence and military units then hunted Saddam Hussein, his two sons, and fifty of his closest henchmen, incarcerating or killing nearly all of them.

With the principal bases of elite and regime power—the Ba'ath Party and the military—destroyed, chaos, but certainly not democracy, ensued. The U.S. measures unbalanced Iraq's ethnic mosaic severely. Ba'athist political and military leaders who managed to flee to Syria before and after the U.S. invasion joined cashiered military officers and leaders of Sunni tribes to launch a deadly insurgency. Combatting the insurgency eventually cost the U.S. military 5,500 dead and 40,000 physically and mentally wounded (many grievously), in addition to several hundred thousand Iraqis dead. The immediate fiscal cost to the United States was about $750 billion, although estimates of the long-term cost ranged toward $3 trillion.

After the Saddam apple cart was overturned by force, it proved exceedingly difficult to build a democratic replacement due to implacable hatreds and distrusts between Iraqi leaders. Kurdish leaders and their followers in the north soon seceded in all but name, and the theocratic Shi'ite regime in Iran exerted steadily greater influence in Iraq's politics. Internecine power struggles occurred without surcease and irregular seizures or attempted seizures of executive power by sectarian militias were widely feared. Elite disunity made the new Baghdad regime clearly unstable, and annual Freedom House assessments consistently ranked Iraq Not Free. A phased withdrawal of U.S. forces, completed in 2013, opened the door to a takeover of much of central Iraq by the Islamic State of Iraq and Syria (ISIS) in 2014, which was ended two years later only through street-to-street combat in Mosul and a resumption of U.S. bombing. Parliamentary elections in May 2018 were followed during 2019 and 2020 by widespread public protests that were repressed by force. "The real lesson of the past twenty years in Iraq is that the only way to have avoided the calamitous repercussions of regime change would have been to not invade the country in the first place" (Gordon 2020, 143).

Elite and regime change in Afghanistan exhibited close parallels to what happened in Iraq. Inducing democracy was claimed to be a main reason for eliminating the Taliban elite that held sway, albeit not over the whole country, after 1996. Following the 9/11 attacks on New York and Washington, DC, in 2001, the United States demanded that Osama bin Laden and al-Qaeda jihadists harbored by the Taliban government be turned over. When the government refused, the United States invoked a United Nations resolution to launch a bombing campaign that, in collaboration with Northern Alliance warlords and fighters, drove Taliban leaders from power in Kabul and from most of the Pushtun region in the south during the last months of 2001. However, the bulk of the Taliban elite as well as Osama bin Ladin and his jihadists fled to sanctuaries in Pakistan's tribal territories and cities such as Peshawar and Quetta. From there, they launched and directed an insurgency that 150,000 joint U.S.-NATO troops, high-tech weaponry, and vast expenditures on civilian aid projects and military and police training programs were unable to defeat. High-profile assassinations of Afghan political and military leaders were frequent, civilian casualties were enormous, and the U.S. military alone suffered nearly 2,500 dead and many times that number wounded.

Following the Taliban's rout in 2001, a conference under the aegis of the United Nations had appointed a transitional government, and its leader, Hamid Karzai, was elected president in late 2004, after what observers said was comprehensive electoral fraud. A parliament was elected, again with observations of widespread fraud, a year later. As in Iraq, the political executive was at loggerheads with parliament, which was widely seen to be a venue for corrupt wheeling and dealing. Successive presidents had to mollify diverse tribal and financial leaders that include members of their own extended families, leaving money-laundering, opium smuggling, and other criminal activities untouched. Democracy was even less apparent and democratic institutions even more façade-like than in Iraq, with Freedom House consistently classifying Afghanistan Not Free.

The Trump administration in Washington opened negotiations with Taliban representatives during 2019, but the government in Kabul, headed by Asraf Ghani, was excluded from them. In late February 2020, an agreement was reached by which U.S. military forces would leave Afghanistan not later than May 1, 2021, in exchange for a Taliban commitment to negotiate a peace settlement with the Kabul government. During the first months of 2021, however, the Taliban carried out more than five hundred targeted assassinations of government officials, journalists, and other elite and subelite Afghan figures (Filkins 2021). In April 2021, President Biden, who had long regarded U.S. involvement in Afghanistan as probably futile, threw in the "towel" and announced that, regardless of conditions in the country, remaining U.S. forces would be withdrawn by September 11, 2021, exactly twenty years after the original Afghanistan-based attacks on the Twin Towers in New York and the Pentagon in Washington.

On July 3, 2021, evacuation of Bagram Air Base, the nerve center for U.S. and NATO ground and air operations in Afghanistan, was completed in the dead of night. A dissolution of demoralized Afghan security forces ensued, and six weeks later the Taliban entered and took control of Kabul without firing a shot. A frantic, chaotic exodus of Afghans who worked with the United States and others who feared restoration of a theocratic Taliban regime began. Total costs of the twenty-year effort were calculated at $2.3 trillion, the deaths of 7,400 U.S. and NATO soldiers and contractors along with those of 120,000 Afghans.

LIBYA AND SYRIA

In Libya, an insurrection against Moammar el-Gaddafi, his family, and his circle of close advisers and security chiefs began in February 2011. It was greeted with enthusiasm in the United States and Europe as possibly heralding Libya's democratization. The insurrection did not manage to eliminate the Gaddafi elite in any thorough way, however. Instead it initiated a civil war, in which disparate anti-Gaddafi forces under no centralized command battled Gaddafi's army and personal security units for control of cities along the Mediterranean coast. Anti-Gaddafi forces eventually overran Sirte, where Gaddafi was killed on October 20, 2011, and an estimated thirty thousand people died during the battles. Although the superior organization and weaponry of Gaddafi forces were weakened by defections—notably that of Minister of Justice Abdul Jalil—they were defeated mainly by U.N.-sanctioned NATO aircraft and cruise missile strikes that began in mid-March 2011, involved thirty thousand sorties and ten thousand air strikes, and lasted seven months.

In Britain, France, and the United States—the main participants in the air attacks—expectations that removing Gaddafi and his regime might open the way to democracy came to naught when Libya dissolved into a patchwork of tribal- and militia-controlled territories. Since 2014, government power has been contested principally by the U.N.-backed Government of National Accord, based in Tripoli, and the forces of General Khalifa Haftar and his Libyan National Army, currently headquartered in Tobruk. Political infighting and civil warfare have yet to produce a clear victor or anything remotely resembling democracy. Upward of a hundred thousand mercenaries and jihadists roam the country unchecked by either government. "The tragic reality was that Libya was broken and . . . no one had a recipe or the means to put it back together" (Gordon 2020, 201).

A popular uprising that began in March 2011 against the regime led by Bashar al-Assad in Syria was even more enthusiastically applauded in the United States and Europe. Holding government power after a coup led by Hafiz al-Assad, Bashar's father, in November 1970, the elite, to which Hafiz al-Assad steadily added loyal Alawites, ruled with an iron fist for four decades. Like the Sunni elite around Saddam, the elite and regime mainly represented the political dominance of an ethnoreligious minority, the Alawite. There was reason to believe that efforts to overthrow the elite and regime would involve a hecatomb of killing because the Alawite elite, including military leaders, would fight to the death. Indeed, Bashar al-Assad "saw leaving or even sharing power as a certain death sentence" (Gordon 2020, 219). Massive bloodletting that cost at least half a million lives and triggered the flight of several million refugees duly occurred.

The bloodshed and chaos, in which the Islamic State (IS) played an important part until it was routed in 2019 by Kurdish fighters and heavy U.S. bombing of Raqqa, the erstwhile IS capital, persuaded external powers to keep their distance and not intervene militarily in even the limited way Britain, France, and the United States had done in Libya. External involvements were mostly limited to Russia supplying weapons and other materiel to Assad forces and Turkey serving as a conduit for supplies to anti-Assad rebel groups, many of them extremists. Neighboring Jordan served as the primary refuge for millions of Syrians fleeing the fighting. An eight-year effort to get rid of the Assad regime appeared to end in Washington's grudging acceptance that Assad would remain in power (Gordon 2020, 242). But because Syria is a mosaic consisting of Assad forces and loyalists in the country's center, Kurds in the northeast, Alawite along the coast, rebel jihadists on the border with Turkey, and other rebel groups in the southeast, each controlling territory, Syria's de facto disintegration as a national state is likely.

TUNISIA AND EGYPT

Nearly simultaneous revolts against dictatorial regimes in Egypt and Tunisia during the early months of 2011 did not entail the elimination of elites and regimes in either country to any significant extent. To be sure, Hosni Mubarak in Egypt and Zine El-Abidine Ben Ali in Tunisia were driven from power, Mubarak being arrested and eventually tried, and Ben Ali fleeing to Saudi Arabia. Both men headed regimes that stifled opponents, rigged elections, and engaged in many corrupt practices. But while the mass protests that began in January 2011 invoked the language of revolution, Egyptian and Tunisian military elites were the principal agents of change. Without saying so, high-ranking military officers conducted what amounted to coups and took charge until promised transitions to democracy could begin.

Although Tunisian and Egyptian media images were of revolution, the reality was infighting among military and government elite factions. In this respect, the upheavals bore a family resemblance to Latin American regimes that have responded countless times to popular uprisings by replacing dictators and their cliques with juntas. In Egypt and Tunisia, as in all Latin American cases other than the Mexican Revolution (discussed in chapter 2), militaries and their leaderships remained intact and retained the upper hand during and after mass protests (Barany 2011, 26–29). And as in Latin America historically, the Egyptian and Tunisian militaries, along with survivors of the Mubarak and Ben Ali ousters, comprised entrenched elites with which newly unshackled parties and social movements had to work if they were to gain significant influence. In terms of prevailing democratic theory about possibilities for democracy, this looked like a promising situation as, indeed, it eventually turned out to be in South America during the 1980s (Higley and Gunther 1992). However, the Egyptian and Tunisian upheavals were not two peas in a pod; there were important differences between them that contributed to different elite and political outcomes. Because the spark for both upheavals was the self-immolation of a vegetable cart owner, Mohammed Bouazizi, in the impoverished town of Sidi Bouzid, 200 kilometers from Tunis, on December 17, 2010, let us consider Tunisia first.

Tunisia was a protectorate controlled by France between 1883 and national independence in 1956. During that long period, a small and privileged political class developed, from which various leading figures were elected as delegates to the National Assembly in Paris. There they acquired experience of democratic politics during France's Third and Fourth Republics. Much like India under the National Congress Party after independence in 1947, postindependence politics in Tunisia unfolded inside an omnibus party, the Destourian Socialist Party (called after 1988 the Democratic Constitutional Assembly, the RCD), led by the illustrious Habib Bourguiba. Bourguiba created what was in effect a presidential monarchy, in which elite power sharing was not wide and democratic politics were limited but neither were they wholly absent. Said to have become senile, Bourguiba was deposed in 1987 by his vice president and former general, Ben Ali, who had the military elite's support.

Like the military regime in neighboring Algeria, Ben Ali and the elite around him faced spreading Islamist unrest, with efforts to contain Islamists and their sympathizers bringing the Tunisian political class under the thumb of the regime and its secret police. Secular critics and opposition parties were allowed limited public expression, some participation in elections, and seats in the RCD-controlled parliament, but the regime had a distinctly autocratic cast. Ben Ali was elected president four times with little or no real opposition, and he was elected for what proved a fifth and last time in 2009, garnering slightly less than 90 percent of all ballots cast, with the RCD winning 161 of the 214 seats in the House of Representatives.

Sparked by Mohammed Bouazizi's suicide, mass protests mushroomed in early 2011 and forced Ben Ali to depart for Saudi Arabia, from where he resigned the presidency on January 14, 2011. Although some fighting among pro– and anti–Ben Ali military units took place, by and large the military elite remained intact. In accordance with the constitution, a state of emergency was declared, and the Constitutional Court affirmed an acting president who presided over a caretaker government. Mohammed Ghannouchi, Ben Ali's long-serving prime minister, led the caretaker government in the same capacity, and his cabinet contained five key ministers belonging to the RCD. Amid continuing protests, however, the RCD ministers resigned a few days later, as did Ghannouchi in late February 2011, with the RCD officially dissolved in early March. Elections for a constituent assembly were announced and then held in late October 2011. The Islamist Renaissance Party (Nahda) won a plurality of votes and assembly seats and a human rights activist, Dr. Moncef Marzouki, was elected interim president until a new constitution could be designed and ratified. Parliamentary elections were held in 2013 and at regular intervals since.

The Tunisian upheaval thus had few earmarks of a genuine revolution. No government collapse occurred, military and police forces did not disintegrate, and mobs meting out "street justice" to anyone suspected of being an elite member were absent. A subsequent U.N. fact-finding commission concluded, however, that some three hundred deaths occurred, with another seven hundred persons injured. An unknown but probably significant number of the deaths and injuries resulted from gunfights between military units and Ben Ali's presidential guard. In any event, secular elite persons and leaders of the ostensibly moderate Islamist Renaissance Party confronted the more radically Islamist Salafis. The confrontation spawned violence by Salafis demanding the imposition and strict application of Sharia law. With the official unemployment rate at 12 percent of the workforce and the real rate probably double that, a swelling of Salafi ranks seemed likely.

Consistent with the discussion of imperfectly unified elites in chapter 1, the question was whether secular and moderate Islamist elite factions would constitute a de facto winning electoral coalition that would induce more radical Islamists, over the course of several election cycles, to adopt less dogmatic stances to compete effectively for a plurality or a majority of votes. In large measure, this is what happened: An imperfectly unified elite formed and evolved gradually toward the consensual unified configuration and a relatively stable democracy. From a democratic standpoint, this was obviously a desirable development because grimmer scenarios could well have unfolded: jockeying for power by mutually mistrustful elite factions and an unstable regime wracked by irregular seizures of executive power or fears of them; a deepening economic malaise fueling radical Islamist growth and triggering a preemptive military takeover, as happened in Algeria during 1992; or a civil war won eventually by radical Islamists who might liquidate secular elite members or force them to flee and leave behind a rigidly theocratic regime, as happened eventually in Afghanistan after Russia withdrew its occupying forces at the end of the 1980s. Down to 2021, however, the democratic path, with inevitable stumbles, has been followed to date in Tunisia.

The Egyptian uprising that began within days of the Tunisian uprising bore signs of a different elite outcome. First under Gamal Abdel Nasser after he and fellow officers overthrew the monarchy in 1952, then under Anwar al-Sadat after he ascended to the presidency upon Nasser's death in 1970, and finally under Hosni Mubarak following Sadat's assassination in 1981, what amounted to a military regime was in control of Egypt. Presidential and People's Assembly elections were held but were subject to so much manipulation as to be little more than charades. Starting with the rapprochement between Egypt and Israel engineered by Jimmy Carter in 1978, the United States gave Egypt $1.3 billion in military aid annually. The aid created ties between American and Egyptian military leaderships, and it can be speculated that the ties helped dissuade Egyptian military leaders from responding more forcibly to mass protests against the Mubarak regime that began on January 25, 2011.

During the following two weeks, swelling crowds of protestors in Cairo, Alexandria, and other cities forced Mubarak to resign from the presidency. On February 11, Mubarak's vice president and former head of the Intelligence Directorate, Omar Suleiman, announced that governing power would henceforth be exercised by the Supreme Council of the Armed Forces (SCAF), whose most senior officer, Field Marshal Mohammed Hussein Tantawi, would be the effective head of state. Tantawi then suspended the constitution, dissolved parliament, and appointed a caretaker government consisting of Mubarak's ministers until elections could be arranged. A year of mass protests and confrontations with police and army units ensued, during which approximately one thousand people died and six thousand were injured, before a parliament was elected in January 2012. In June 2012, Mohammed Morsi, a man associated with the Muslim Brotherhood, narrowly defeated Ahmed Shafik, Mubarak's last prime minister, in a presidential runoff election.

Forty-eight hours before results of the runoff election were to be announced, SCAF ordered parliament closed after the Supreme Constitutional Court, consisting mostly of justices appointed by Mubarak, ruled that the law under which parliament had been elected six months earlier was invalid. SCAF simultaneously arrogated all legislative power to itself and issued edicts that greatly limited presidential authority. Two weeks after he was declared to have won the presidency, however, Morsi ordered parliament to reconvene, which it did for a symbolic seven minutes on July 10 without military interference. What appeared to be a standoff between Morsi and SCAF took place until, in early August, Morsi cited the killing of fifteen Egyptian soldiers by alleged jihadists in the Sinai Desert as a reason for securing the resignations of Tantawi and several of his SCAF colleagues. Morsi replaced Tantawi with a younger general, Abdel

Fattah al-Sisi, who was believed to hold views, especially views skeptical of U.S. involvements in the Middle East, not antagonistic to Brotherhood leaders.

Many observers speculated that a deal between Morsi and SCAF had been struck. Said to have been negotiated directly by Morsi with younger SCAF generals, the deal allegedly traded a restoration of parliament and presidential authority, plus the military's acceptance of a large role for Brotherhood leaders in designing a constitution, in exchange for promotions of younger field-grade officers, the military's immunity from prosecutions for actions during the mass protests, plus the military's untrammeled control of the defense budget and extensive economic enterprises. After the Constitutional Court invalidated alleged understandings between the two most powerful elite camps in post-Mubarak Egypt—the military and the Brotherhood—a military coup led by al-Sisi overthrew Morsi in July 2013. He and other Brotherhood leaders were arrested, tried, and imprisoned, and Morsi died in custody in June 2019.

It was tempting to interpret the dramatic Egyptian events during 2011–2012 as indicating a sudden and basic elite settlement of the kind outlined in chapter 1. Most of the conditions for a settlement appeared to exist: (1) two well-articulated and powerful elite camps—the SCAF and the Brotherhood—with a history of deep mistrust and the capacity to hurt each other seriously; (2) a triggering crisis in the form of the SCAF's abrupt dissolution of parliament and arrogation of legislative and executive power to itself; (3) rapid and apparently face-to-face secret negotiations among uppermost leaders of the two camps before word leaked out and other groups mobilized to torpedo any deal between them; and (4) formal announcement of a deal in the form of public resignations by Tantawi and other generals capped by a ceremony awarding them Egypt's highest honor, the Collar of the Nile.

Yet a crucial condition for an elite settlement—established, experienced, and skilled leaders with enough authority to bring recalcitrant elite persons and followers along—was not satisfied. Morsi was a man of limited political experience even if other Brotherhood leaders were political veterans; the newly promoted SCAF leaders were young, untested politically, and their control of the military was uncertain. In Egypt's superheated political arena, many others were eager to grab the brass ring. Viewed through the prism of chapter 1, Egypt was at a relatively high level of socioeconomic development, elites were large and no longer isolated from non-elites, and numerous elite actors gave their first allegiance to the partisan interests of the organizations and interests they led. These factors tended to rule out an elite settlement. The consequence has been a continuation of elite disunity and an unstable authoritarian regime.

REFLECTIONS

The belief that eliminating or crippling elites opens the way to democracy is widespread but simplistic. In unchecked elite power struggles—the typical situation in most societies today and during modern history—a distinction between good and bad elites has little meaning. From the standpoint of each elite person or faction, everyone else is up to no good. This is not to deny that from a normative democratic standpoint there are noxious tyrants like Saddam Hussein and Moammar Gadaffi, along with the Adolf Hitlers and Joseph Stalins of this world (Snyder 2017). Such tyrants are flatly incompatible with democratic values, and their elimination is an essential first step in pursuing those values. But in complex modern societies tyrants are never lone actors; they depend on and are embedded in elites, and the wisdom of getting rid of such elites when getting rid of tyrants is not so obvious. Eliminating ruling elites, I have tried to suggest, seldom brings political improvement; chaos, during which many innocent bystanders perish, is more likely. Collaboration between elite individuals and factions who regard each other as unsavory is part and parcel of the ways in which consensual unified elites form and function.

Innocent of specialist knowledge that would no doubt force alterations, I have painted with a broad brush to examine overthrows of autocratic regimes in Iraq, Afghanistan, Libya, Tunisia, and Egypt. The autocratic Syrian regime headed by Bashar al-Assad has stopped at nothing to kill and drive out opponents. If the regime were somehow toppled, political and territorial disintegration analogous to that which followed the toppling of the Gadaffi regime in Libya would probably ensue. Where elites associated with autocratic regimes were driven out (Iraq and Afghanistan) or dispersed (Libya), little good has come of it. Sectarian and region-based warfare continues in all three countries, tens of thousands of lives have been lost, all three countries seem dangerously near territorial breakup, and external efforts to induce democracy, particularly in Iraq and Afghanistan, have incurred huge costs with little success.

Overthrows of Tunisian and Egyptian autocrats have not, so far, had similar consequences. This is primarily because no liquidation of elites surrounding Ben Ali and Mubarak occurred. Quite the opposite: elites survived largely intact and provided leaders of transitional regimes. In Tunisia, this set the stage for protracted pushing and shoving between secular and Islamist elite factions, with the military elite acting as a balance wheel or mediator. It is not altogether implausible to speculate that repeated electoral contests won by moderate secular leaders and Islamist parties might facilitate a gradual convergence toward a consensual unified elite adhering to norms of political restraint. In Egypt, promising signs of a basic accommodation between the main post-Mubarak elite camps did not come to fruition, mainly for want of able leaders and probably also because the complexity of Egypt and ties between elites and nonelites stand in the way.

The Arab Spring folly has one other aspect worth noting. This is the premise, which is a shibboleth of democratic ideology and contemporary social science, that democracy is created by the *demos*— by non-elites. Rising mass participation in politics, which is said to be a consequence of economic development and "modernization," is believed to lead, at least in the proverbial long run, to democratic institutions. Popular uprisings during the Arab Spring were widely seen as manifestations of this shibboleth and were joyfully applauded as such. They led, however, to catastrophe except where, in Tunisia, elites remained largely intact and inclined to collaborate in keeping the genie of non-elite unrest bottled up.

Chapter Six

Political Realism in the Twenty-First Century

Contrary to what most Americans and other Westerners have believed, politics are almost entirely a relativistic universe in the sense that there is no universal standard to which political actions can be made to conform. As stated in the introduction, the only product of politics that can usually be recognized as of some value by most people is a minimal amount of organized peace—some outer limit on the pursuit of conflict in society. Where politics have long been organized and practiced along representative lines, and where economic and social conditions are essentially benign, there *may* be a somewhat more substantial general interest. Most persons might agree that the objective merit of representative politics is that it makes acquiescing in policies of which one disapproves easier because there is some chance of changing them by peaceful means. But even a representative government is to some degree imposed on most citizens.

How does one find a place to stand in this relativistic political universe? Normally, a person's circumstances give her or him a general orientation toward political matters. One's social position leads to preferring some values instead of others. Thus, middle-class persons who wish to make, or must make, reliable plans for future actions usually condemn strikes that disrupt provisions of goods and services and interfere with their plans. By the same token, factory workers engaged in repetitive, personally unplanned work often conclude that their interests can best be advanced through strikes, and they are likely to condone them. So, are politics merely a matter of self-interest, and are all bases of moral choice illusions?

Not completely because the political orientation of each person is not equally important and relevant in politics. Usually, those whose orientations are most closely based on self-interest or the narrow prejudices of a specific social stratum or ethnoreligious, regional, or other category do not have much influence if there are considerable numbers of more broadly oriented elite persons around. By manipulating the political agenda, inhibiting mass mobilizations, and forestalling the emergence of conflicts through clever planning, such elites may prevent the nihilistic potential of politics from becoming manifest. It is only when there are no such elites, or when they are for some reason incapable of managing politics in these ways, that the situation is very nearly hopeless.

WANING OPTIMISM

Two basic circumstances during the eighteenth and nineteenth centuries created a principled optimism about political and social life in the leading Western societies. First, after about 1700 and until the Great Depression of the 1930s, the running together of clever artisanship, scientific reasoning, and readily available land and other natural resources supported the agreeable notion that increases in economic productivity would eventually meet the needs of people in Western societies on a substantially equal basis. Second, from the defeat of invading Turk forces in front of Vienna in 1683 until World War II, the clear military superiority of Western countries over the rest of the world encouraged people in them to presume that they would never be faced with the threat of cultural degradation, enslavement, or extermination at the hands of a non-Western power.

These circumstances had a profound impact on how elites and other influential persons thought about politics and society. Expectations about the long-term equalizing effects of material progress led them to suppose that radically different definitions of social justice would eventually be joined in a synthesis acceptable to all.

The sense of safety from conquest by a non-Western power allowed them to believe that conflicts in the pursuit of social justice could be fully explored, exploited, and fought out without risking the loss of one's own culture. The rise to a principled optimism was reflected in the idealism of Locke, the utopianism of Rousseau and the early socialists, and then the full panoply of progressive liberal, democratic, and socialist thought during the nineteenth century. Because of their uniquely favored historical experience and geographic safety, Americans were especially inclined toward optimism.

By the twentieth century's start, personal safety and respectful treatment in most of life's contingencies were assured to members of upper- and middle-class families in Western Europe, the countries settled by English-speaking peoples, and in the larger cities of Eastern Europe and Latin America. Even in African, Asian, and Middle Eastern colonial territories ruled by Europeans, this was generally true for most upper- and middle-class persons without European ancestors, although the privileges of European rulers were embarrassing and humiliating to recently arrived "native" families. Among the well behaved, well dressed, and well spoken in all these countries and territories, Western liberal conceptions of personal dignity and impartial justice were generally professed and broadly observed.

Around 1900, of course, such treatment did not extend in any large measure to members of lower-class families, racial or ethnic minorities, and women who acted outside of traditional female roles. Especially in countries and territories not directly influenced by British political practices, and especially when they asserted "rights" that dominant classes and social strata did not think they had, persons in lower statuses were not reliably respected. There is no reason to suppose, however, that they were less respected or less safe from abuses than such persons had been throughout all earlier history. On the contrary, the widespread profession of liberal values among the well off resulted in the relatively respectful treatment of the less well off in many legal and work situations. In general, much larger proportions of non-elites were accorded respect by authorities and institutions than ever before. This meant that larger proportions of non-elites than ever before lived lives of substantial self-respect.

In about 1900, governments in Western Europe and the countries settled by English-speaking peoples derived much of their legitimacy from public elections of representative parliaments and legislatures. To be sure, monarchs in Denmark, Germany, Italy, Sweden, and the Low Countries claimed significant degrees of independent power, and monarchs in Austria-Hungary, Portugal, and Spain wielded such power. Nevertheless, the liberal idea of political choices by at least moderately large electorates in real party competitions was the prevailing standard of political authority, and in most Western countries there was no expectation that military coups were likely to veto choices made by voters. Although this liberal political standard did not extend much beyond Western Europe and the English-speaking countries, political activists in other parts of the globe tended to accept representative government as their preferred political model. In part, of course, this reflected Western colonial power. But whatever the cause, liberal political principles were dominant intellectually, and liberal practices were beginning to spread widely in 1900.

The period around 1900 can well be seen, in retrospect, as the high-water mark in the advance of liberal practices. Not long after 1900, serious interruptions of those practices occurred in many Western countries. Austria, Belgium, Denmark, Finland, France, Germany, Italy, the Netherlands, Norway, Portugal, and Spain all experienced the suppression of liberal practices for substantial periods before, during, or after World War II. For much of the twentieth century, moreover, Russia, China, and several other countries professed communist principles that in practice disregarded the personal rights involved in liberalism, and they eschewed meaningful electoral contests and choices.

Today, unlike in 1900, no Western country exerts much political influence and power outside the West except, insofar as raw military power goes, the United States, and recent developments suggest that U.S. power, not to mention U.S. influence, is in decline. Except in Japan, South Korea, and a few scattered ex-British colonies, such as Barbados, Ghana, and Jamaica, liberal practices are precarious at best. It is certainly no longer the case that members of upper- and middle-class families are assured of safety and respectful treatment in the cities of Latin America, Africa, the Middle East, and South and Southeast Asia. In the face of criminal and political kidnapping and terrorist actions on a scale unknown since the Middle Ages, the safety and personal liberty of educated, wealthy, and politically prominent persons and families are frequently at risk. As they were historically before the rise of Western societies to global dominance, politics in much of the world are again a dangerous but unavoidable activity. They tend to degrade, humiliate, and not infrequently destroy all but the most fortunate of those who engage in them.

When traveling outside the West and even when at home, Westerners are no longer exempt from murderous terrorist actions and the taking of hostages. Especially when outside the West, elite and other influential Westerners such as business leaders and journalists can no longer count on personal safety and respectful treatment. Enmeshed in elaborate security arrangements, they face the real, if statistically remote, possibility of being killed, maimed, or held hostage in the interest of some local political sect's public relations, money-making efforts, or vendetta. The machine gunning of a score of Westerners in Mumbai's most expensive hotels during December 2008 is but one example. The 9/11 attacks on New York and Washington, DC, and multiple terrorist attacks in European and Antipodean cities have shown that Western countries face powerful foes, some of which are fanatically anti-Western and capable of inflicting devastation on Western populations, no matter how suicidal and "irrational" such attacks might seem.

Manifested by the relatively illiberal surveillance, profiling, and other security measures Western governments have lately instituted, this new vulnerability of Westerners tends to weaken liberal attitudes and practices. Historic liberal protections of individual rights, such as habeas corpus, are loosened, while what a recent U.S. vice president termed a "Dark Side" involving harsh interrogation, torture, and even assassination of suspected subversives and commanders of hostile forces is increasingly regarded by Western elites and governments as a necessary evil.

The basic political reason why liberal practices have failed to spread much beyond the comparatively few countries that enjoyed them 120 years ago has been the failure of consensual unified elites to form in most countries of the world. As adumbrated in chapter

1, a consensually unified, or at least an imperfectly unified, elite must emerge before a stable representative government conducive to substantial and sustained political freedom and meaningful political choice becomes possible. Around 1900, consensually unified elites existed in about ten Western countries. Although they exist in perhaps thirty countries today, nearly all are in Europe or the Anglosphere (Higley and Burton 2006, 33–54).

Recent Western political thought has generally failed to recognize the elite basis of stable representative government. Instead it has naïvely urged universal suffrage, free and fair elections, respect for human rights, and adoption of fully democratic constitutions on all countries of the world, in most of which elites are deeply disunified with many of their members engaged in dog-eat-dog struggles for political survival, Much too blithely, recent Western thought has assumed, as it did in the "Arab Spring folly," that simply by adopting representative institutions and practices countries will move from unstable and illiberal regimes to reasonably stable democracies. The failure to recognize the elite basis of stable democracy reflects the unrealistic assumption that political possibilities are open ended. It also reflects, as discussed in chapter 4, a conflation of ultimate liberal and instrumental democratic values that should be kept separate and distinct.

Western societies may continue to enjoy important advantages over the rest of the world for much of the present century, yet there is no general ground for assuming this. Despite domestic dissension, they may be able to defend themselves against non-Western threats to their security, but this is not self-evident. It may happen that increases in Western economic productivity will be large enough to buy off domestic discontents through relatively painless distributions out of an economic surplus, but there is no reason to take this for granted. If the ways people think about politics and society reflect their basic circumstances, these uncertainties will give rise to outlooks much less optimistic than those that flourished two and three centuries ago in Western societies.

To sustain these societies between now and the middle of this century (beyond which Western circumstances and those of the wider world are largely unforeseeable), there is no realistic alternative to elites conducting what will amount to a *holding operation* aimed at husbanding the powers and political practices of Western societies. As Samuel Huntington put it when concluding *The Clash of Civilizations*, "The principal responsibility of Western leaders . . . is not to attempt to reshape other civilizations, but to preserve, protect, and renew the unique qualities of Western civilization" (1996, 311). A holding operation will not involve a neat package of policies about which all or most elites and influential persons agree. Nor will it conform to a "West versus the Rest" scenario. Rather, it will involve a sharper understanding by elites and educated circles about the need to cope collectively with a dangerous world and with domestic conditions that are no longer progressing. It will entail recognizing twenty-first-century political realities and what is and is not possible in politics.

REALISM ABROAD

A generally high living standard has been the most distinctive feature of the leading Western societies for at least the past 150 years. After World War II, the standard became so high and general that observers began to speak, as did the American economist John Kenneth Galbraith somewhat ironically, about "the affluent society" (1958). Accompanying this high standard were many qualities of life that thoughtful persons were inclined to treat as ultimate goods: safety from interpersonal violence, wide educational opportunities, and a feeling that one's views and wishes are reflected in a representative political process through which public policies are determined. As unique historically as the prosperity that facilitated and made them possible, these refinements of life afforded greater self-respect and dignity to a larger proportion of populations in the leading Western countries than was ever the case in another civilization (Huntington 1996).

After recovery from World War II, the spread of optimistic views among elites and educated strata led many to devalue those advantages and press for major changes of a broadly egalitarian or laissez-faire kind. But while it is easy enough to imagine a society in which everyone would feel socially equal or ambitiously entrepreneurial and at the same time be free and fully allegiant politically, even in imagination it is not possible to fill in the details of such a society if one simultaneously presumes modern urbanism, large and impersonal organization, science, and complex technology. It is part of the unrealistic hubris with which elites and educated persons have viewed the world that many have spoken as though such a society is in fact attainable.

The problem is that one can sharply condemn the inequalities; marginal social statuses of many persons; bothersome government regulations; anemic rates of economic growth; racial, ethnic, and gender discriminations; and other shortcomings perceived to afflict Western societies only by invoking a completely imaginary ideal as the standard for comparison. If, by contrast, one undertakes a real comparison with other urbanized societies, past or present, it is impossible not to recognize the unprecedented advantages that Western societies have afforded very large proportions, although by no means all, of their members.

A refrain in public discussion has been whether Western populations deserve their advantages. The answer must be that in any meaningful sense of personal merit, neither present Western generations nor those of the recent past clearly "deserve" the greater affluence, human rights, health care, and numerous other advantages they enjoy. Some in Western societies have been kind, some have been prudent, and some have been honest, but some have been bullies and not a few have been thieves. As I have tried to show elsewhere (Higley 2016, 41–98), all one can broadly say is that through force of circumstance and without ever clearly foreseeing the conditions to which their collective conduct was leading, Westerners followed the motives and did the things that brought them their recent and present advantages. It must be admitted that, except sometimes in warfare or rebellion, relatively few made serious voluntary sacrifices to improve the human lot.

This means that if there could be a deliberate sharing of the most central and distinctive cultural traits of Western societies with the world's population, or if the organization and functioning of Western politics and societies could be deliberately shared with all those in the world who have not been part of them, there would be no substantial moral grounds for refusing to apportion Western advantages globally. However, neither selected cultural traits nor the components of ongoing political systems and societies can be parceled out. Only their material products—goods and various services—could be allocated more equally, either through voluntary donations or through payments of tribute. But redistributing material goods and services to the rest of the world would not reliably spread the essential and valuable aspects of Western political behavior, especially elite behavior. If some workers in non-Western countries get a little more money to spend because of Western donations or tribute, they do not at the same time acquire Western attitudes toward work, human dignity, and personal independence. By the same token, if elites and upper-class persons in non-Western countries obtain sumptuous homes, private airplanes, access to exclusive resorts, and other luxuries based on Western donations or tribute, there is no reason to suppose that they thereby absorb Western proclivities toward individual prudence, reasonably honest business practices, and respect for civil liberties.

On the contrary, if donations or tribute were seen as acts of Western weakness or placation, providing them would reinforce the already strong tendency in relatively impoverished, politically unstable societies to regard extortion and graft as the normal ways in which persons and countries advance themselves. At least, it is difficult to see how merely sharing Western societies' material abundance more equally would over any reasonable length of time foster an acceptance of the complicated ways of exchanging mutual satisfactions that have flourished in them. Not only might the more equal distribution of material possessions throughout the world discourage Westernization but ultimate and instrumental liberal values in Western societies would likely be undermined. Because these ultimate values—personal safety, political representation, civil liberties—depend in considerable measure on affluence for their workings, any large redistribution of Western wealth and material possessions on a world basis would lessen or destroy them. At the same time, and for reasons given throughout this book, it is unlikely that these ultimate values would be recreated in most non-Western countries.

Between now and mid-century, therefore, Western societies have no obligation to share their resources and advantages beyond normal acts of charity in the face of calamities and beyond negotiated or unavoidable concessions in world public health and commerce. If anything, they have a positive obligation to defend, insofar as they can, what is already theirs. As Huntington concluded, elites have an obligation to preserve those central aspects of Western societies that have been broadly beneficial for their populations. Within practical limits, it is incumbent on Western elites and countries to support and defend each other against non-Western encroachments and accept into the Western fraternity only countries that seem securely within the tradition of personal independence, limited political power, and respect for human rights that are the essence of Western practices.

Current and foreseeable political and social conditions in the bulk of non-Western countries make Western countries' close relations with them inadvisable. The most important political condition is elite disunity. This is widespread and there is no reason to think that it will become much less prevalent during the next several decades. It appears, nevertheless, that approximations of consensual unified or imperfectly unified elites exist in a score of non-Western countries, although these approximations are in nearly all cases recent and have not stood the test of time. In Latin America, the peaceful give-and-take characteristic of mutually trusting elites seems to keep politics somewhat restrained in Chile, Colombia, Costa Rica, Mexico, Uruguay, and perhaps in Argentina and in Brazil once Jair Bolsonaro and his military clique depart executive power. In the Caribbean, Barbados, the Dominican Republic, and Jamaica have reasonably peaceful politics, as do Botswana, Ghana, Morocco, Senegal, South Africa, and possibly Kenya and Tunisia in Africa. Bhutan, India, Malaysia, and Singapore in South and Southeast Asia, and Japan, South Korea, Taiwan (so long as it remains de facto independent of China), and maybe Mongolia in East Asia are also marked by significant degrees of elite cooperation to keep politics tame. But nearly everywhere else, elite disunity guarantees severe conflicts that force individual leaders and cliques to concentrate on their own survival instead of making prudent assessments of their countries' difficulties and needs.

There is little or nothing that Western governments can do diplomatically or through loans and subventions that will alter the unstable character of regimes in countries with disunified elites. As the United States recently tried to do militarily in Afghanistan and Iraq, a Western government can help one rival faction prevail over others, but this is unlikely to have long-term benefits for the government that acts in this way. Nothing a Western government does is likely to improve the human rights record or win the affection or allegiance of such countries on anything like a lasting basis. Treating a country with disunified elites as an ally means deferring to the frequently desperate circumstances, fears, and practices of its most powerful elite factions, while at the same time chiding its government for violating democratic practices and human rights. As will happen to the Biden administration for "abandoning" recently liberated women in Afghanistan, this can only discredit a Western government in the eyes of numerous groups at home who are inclined to make moral judgments about the shape of things in the world.

Here is one basic aspect of political realism abroad during the next several decades. Western countries cannot afford close relations with countries whose elites are disunified. Close relations not only discredit Western governments but, as the aftermath of the Shah's overthrow in Iran has shown, they make getting along with successor regimes difficult. Between now and mid-century, elites and governments in Western countries must accept that there is no way in which they can effectively prevent countries with disunified elites from coming under the control of unsavory elite factions and regimes.

Avoiding close relations with such countries does not mean allowing *jihadi* and other fervently anti-Western groups to spread unchecked. Across the Sahel from Senegal to Sudan, and in some areas of central Africa such as northeastern Nigeria, Western intelligence and military contingents will have to be deployed selectively to support local and African Union forces battling jihadi insurgents. France's positioning of a limited number of special military units in and around Chad, its former colony, to help check Islamic State and al-Qaeda advances is an example, as is deployment of several hundred U.S. soldiers and airmen to help hold Al-Shabab at bay in

Somalia. Important for keeping the world from becoming "the West versus the Rest," such deployments must not, however, evolve into futile nation-building projects or defenses of extant regimes at all costs.

Ultimately, Western countries cannot expect, realistically, to retain all the resources and other advantages they earlier obtained economically, militarily, and politically. Once a shakeout period ends, they will be somewhat poorer, at least relatively, and perhaps even absolutely. But in view of disunified elites, cultural dispositions, deep ethnoreligious cleavages, large surplus working-age populations, as well as usually small shares of world resources and the depredations of climate change and disease pandemics, most non-Western countries will probably not be a great deal richer than at present. This ignores, of course, the disaster of a war in which China or some other non-Western power presses a bid for international hegemony. It is virtually certain that the consequence of a war over hegemony would be a permanent and worldwide retrogression from early twenty-first-century economic and other standards of life.

REALISM AT HOME

The insecurity of work and the consequent demoralization, disaffection, diseases of despair, and millenarian pursuits among steadily larger segments of non-elites in Western societies, discussed in chapter 3, can probably be counteracted only through a combination of two eventualities. One is lower population growth that in time makes Western population sizes more proportionate to the number of jobs that advanced postindustrial economies need to have performed. Their inability to organize existing populations effectively argues for lower future growth. This means making all practical means of birth control, including abortion, readily available; adjusting tax laws and subsidies to not penalize married or unmarried but childless persons and encourage small families; and curtailing legal immigration and severely inhibiting illegal immigration. Such measures will be abhorrent to many persons and morally agonizing for elites to implement. Consequently, much political skill and courage on the part of elites and authorities charged with devising and enforcing relevant laws and policies will be needed.

The other eventuality is the emergence of a recognized need for new and reasonably attractive jobs to accomplish things that are at present not accomplished or are accomplished inadequately. Such jobs can be created most readily in the general area of ecological, environmental, and public health safeguards, involving measures and actions to expand and modernize infrastructure, control pollution, slow and offset the effects of climate change, guard against disease epidemics, and conserve scarce resources. More people trained and employed by governments will be needed to plan, regulate, and coordinate these safeguards. In addition, as threats of cyber- and other attacks by domestic and foreign terrorists heighten, the need for police persons, guards, inspectors, and specialists in tracking communications and other forms of surveillance will increase. So too will the need for scientists and medical practitioners skilled in identifying and combating disease pandemics that tend to originate in non-Western countries where the infrastructures and personnel necessary to prevent or contain them are lacking.

However, neither a restraint of population growth nor a creation of additional forms of necessary, or at least useful, employment can be expected to occur soon. Indeed, it is unlikely that the individual incentives and political support needed for population restraint will form, and it is possible that it would, in any case, be offset by further automation of work tasks. Thus, the most realistic way to shore up Western societies by the middle of this century is to expand environmental and resource conservation as well as human service occupations, not only for their own merits but also to check the spread of demoralization, disaffection, and millenarianism among non-elites. To pay for this expansion, carbon and other environmentally protective taxes will be necessary: on motor vehicle purchases, fuels, and road usage; subsidies for electric vehicle purchases and recharging stations; removal of subsidies for fossil fuel industries; luxury surcharges on travels and homes of the wealthy; and a variety of other revenue-increasing measures—for example, supplementing personal income taxation with a comprehensive value-added tax in the United States.

Between now and this century's mid-point, elites and others with influence will have to recognize that many persons who are insecure, demoralized, and disaffected cannot be reabsorbed into Western workforces and that it is necessary to tolerate this problem while trying to prevent its further spread. This will require a much sharper awareness of the limits to social reform and necessitate an implicit holding operation. Skillful management of tensions and conflicts by elites more conscious of their pivotal roles and responsibilities than at present will be essential.

THE OUTLOOK

There are signs that a holding operation by Western elites and governments between now and mid-century is not unrealistic. In the wake of the United Kingdom's departure, the European Union appears to move in the quasi-federal direction that British governments always opposed. An important step has been the Union's adoption of a 750-billion-Euro "solidarity fund" involving the issuance of common debt. Aimed at recovering from the Coronavirus pandemic, which has been suffered more or less uniformly by member states, the solidarity fund is an advance toward European federalism. It is accompanied by mounting elite discussion of the European Union's need for "strategic autonomy" as an integrated diplomatic, military, and technological force in the global arena. Yet abrasions between member states and the European Commission over the supply of vaccines to counter the Coronavirus pandemic are reminders that competing national interests are hardly relics of the past in Europe.

On both sides of the Atlantic, the Coronavirus pandemic's public health, economic, and social ravages have muted populist nationalism. Measures to combat the pandemic muffle issues, such as the unauthorized mass migrations that populist-nationalist politicians, parties, and governments have exploited. At present, the political standings of Alternative for Germany, The League in Italy, Forum for Democracy in the Netherlands, Vox in Spain, the Sweden Democrats, and those of populist-nationalist governments in Poland and

Hungary have sagged, although Marine Le Pen's and her National Rally's chances in France's 2022 elections should not be underestimated. In Britain, Boris Johnson's fumbling response to the pandemic cast doubt on his policymaking competence. With 150,000 dead by April 2021, Britain had one of the highest pandemic mortality rates in the world. In addition, when the thin gruel extracted by Johnson from protracted Brexit negotiations with the European Union becomes apparent—especially the lack of favorable terms for Britain's crucial financial industry and the ambiguous economic status of Northern Ireland—his electoral prospects may dim while prospects of Scotland joining the European Union and Northern Ireland merging with the Irish Republic will brighten. If still prime minister after the 2024 elections, Johnson may have the dubious distinction of presiding over the United Kingdom's disintegration.

In the United States, mismanagement of the response to the pandemic contributed to Donald Trump's defeat in the November 2020 presidential election. His refusal to accept defeat and his efforts to overturn the election culminated in the violent January 6, 2021, assault on the Capitol by a mob of Trump supporters, with members of Congress and Trump's vice president escaping harm at the hands of the mob by minutes. A week later, the Democratic majority in the House of Representatives, joined by ten Republicans, voted to impeach Trump for "incitement of insurrection." However, the constitutionally required two-thirds of Senate members necessary to convict an impeached president could not be obtained, and Trump was, for the second time in a year, acquitted on February 13, 2021, despite seven Republican senators and all fifty Democratic senators voting to convict him.

Climaxing four years of elite, media, and political party polarization centered on Trump's presidential behavior and policies, these febrile events raised questions about one of this book's central contentions, namely, that within a specified universe of discourse consensual unified elites like the American are reliably self-perpetuating. Consequently, irregular seizures or attempted seizures of executive power are not observed, and the functioning of established political institutions is not interrupted. The January 6 assault on the Capitol was widely portrayed as an "attempted coup," although the several thousand Trump supporters who for a few hours stormed through the halls of Congress had no clear leaders and no plan for an alternative government. Claiming to follow instructions given by Trump in his incendiary speech immediately before they marched to the Capitol, the bulk of the mob believed their purpose was to stop Congress from certifying Electoral College votes declaring Joe Biden the duly elected forty-sixth president. The assault on the Capitol was insurrectionary, but it was not an attempted irregular seizure of executive power.

Yet the January insurrection had a sobering effect on elites. Condemnation of congressional members' brush with personal harm and subsequent threats of harm to some members and their families was nearly universal. A serious split in the Republican Party elite between Trump and anti-Trump factions became evident. To ensure a peaceful inauguration of Biden as president on January 20, overwhelming military and police force was summoned to surround the Capitol. With fifty years of experience in national-level electoral politics and office holding, Biden's political proclivities were those typical of consensual unified elite practices: bargaining and compromise; technical and procedural feasibilities instead of ultimate rights and wrongs; restrained partisanship; subordinating one's own quirks and foibles to the existing structure of power; depicting allies and opponents as well-intentioned even if sometimes mistaken; praising the society's core political, economic, and social values; and calling for political unity at every turn. Installed in the White House, Biden sought to shore up these and other aspects of consensual elite unity, although he of course did not speak openly in such "elitist" terms. Manifested by the relief with which governing and other elites in nearly all Western countries greeted Biden's presidency, the need for elite consensus and unity was recognized more openly across the West.

It is uncertain, however, if elites in Western countries can perpetuate unity and consensus, and thus political stability, in the decades ahead. Disease pandemics, climate change, racial and ethnic grievances, mass migrations from outside the West, as well as the ease with which fevered conspiratorial beliefs spread through social media may prove beyond elite management. Fissures within elites and between them and segments of non-elites are fraught, and they portend considerable social disorder and political incivility. In the United States, failure to contain these challenges might swing the political pendulum back toward Donald Trump or someone aping him. It cannot be said with confidence that American elite consensus and unity would survive a second Trump presidency or that of a Trump clone.

Epilogue

The American Preoccupation with Non-Elites

This book has contended that the internal workings, commitments, and actions of national elites constitute the basic distinctions to be made among the political systems of all independent nation-states. The extent to which elites do or do not trust and cooperate with each other is logically and factually prior to constitutional and institutional arrangements, to the existence of political stability or instability, and to any practical and durable degree of democratic politics. The existence and centrality of elites make all utopias impossible to achieve, and major political change stems mainly from variations in elite relations that take place within wide parameters set by non-elite political orientations. Accordingly, basic choices in politics pertain mainly to the desirability of some kinds of national elites over others and to the wisdom in any concrete situation of trying to modify or transform an existing elite.

American culture has never been hospitable to frankly expressed ideas about the inescapable centrality and importance of elites in politics. Because of their favored historical experience, Americans have always been strongly inclined to think of politics as an unrestricted means for achieving their ideals, and they have prevailingly defined these in terms of a thoroughgoing political equality. As de Tocqueville saw so clearly, democracy has been the touchstone of American culture from the start, and Americans have unhesitatingly assumed that the road to a full measure of it is open ended.

During the early part of the twentieth century, however, the populistic character of American culture had relatively little influence on those who held university positions and engaged in political discussion of a scholarly kind. The serious scholar of that period was conscious of a vague alienation from American culture and a halfhearted identification with European culture—halfhearted because of Europe's seeming penchant for violent nationalisms and dangerous wars. Yet the material and even spiritual advantages promised by the American experience were usually sufficient to discourage expatriation, and most American scholars contented themselves with addressing much the same kind of educated upper-class audience, and in much the same terms, as their European counterparts. Like Europeans, they felt some doubt that America's populistic goals were fully attainable, although this is not to deny that a few of them offered more distinctively American viewpoints in such matters—Charles A. Beard, Vernon Parrington, and perhaps Woodrow Wilson come most readily to mind. On the whole, scholarly approaches to politics did not differ greatly from one side of the Atlantic to the other during the early twentieth century.

Until the advent of the Roosevelt administration, it was much less likely that a serious student of American politics would engage in an active political role than was the case in European countries. Instead of participating in policymaking and statecraft, American scholars devoted themselves to factual writings that described the workings of American political institutions. They were not much concerned with normative questions and almost not at all concerned with any sort of "theory." They had no special need for doctrines, least of all doctrines treating the workings and potentials of avowedly democratic institutions skeptically. While there was some discussion of Robert Michels's "Iron Law of Oligarchy" after he delivered invited lectures at the University of Chicago and Williams College in 1926–1927, the elite-centered writings of Gaetano Mosca and Vilfredo Pareto were not available in English until the second half of the 1930s. Prodigious archival research by Giorgio Volpe (2021), a contemporary Italian scholar, reveals that from 1932 to 1934 Arthur Livingston, an American scholar of Romance languages, conducted a Harvard University graduate seminar about Pareto's untranslated *Treatise on General Sociology* (1916/1935). The seminar contributed to a short-lived "Pareto Vogue" during the 1930s among a small circle of American social scientists and intellectuals seeking an alternative to Marxism, but it had no discernible impact on America's populistic culture.

THE NEW DEAL AND WORLD WAR II

By greatly altering academic career possibilities, the Roosevelt New Deal inaugurated a fundamental shift in the stance of scholars working on politically relevant matters. Starting in 1933, many older scholars became advisers to New Deal politicians or held temporary appointments as government officials. Many young scholars and graduate students moved directly into expanding federal and state bureaucracies. Participation in World War II and the much larger role played by the United States in world affairs after the war accelerated this shift.

Although the emergence of the United States as one of only two countries capable of playing a great power role in world affairs after 1945 was, for most Americans, an unforeseen and undesired development, the country's changed global role, and the military triumphs that ushered it in, served to sweep away most doubts about the efficacies of American political institutions at home and abroad. Skepticism about the more extreme possibilities held out by America's populistic ideals—a skepticism that could be heard in conversations among the educated before the New Deal and the war—ceased to be expressed. With its cessation, the sponsoring of what are today coming to be recognized as utopian goals, such as promoting democracy around the world and implanting it in many non-Western countries while abolishing poverty and righting many wrongs at home, became endemic.

A changed role for intellectuals in American society was one aspect of this shift. Objectively, intellectuals became highly influential on many public matters. Subjectively, those who held important academic, bureaucratic, and literary positions became very conscious of their influence. In helping to produce large numbers of new intellectuals as the size of the educated public increased markedly with the great postwar expansion of higher education, leading intellectuals made little or no effort to reproduce the modest attitudes about political possibilities that had been a feature of educated circles earlier in the century. Facing the new tasks of leading other nations in public policy, American intellectuals now saw themselves as required to act, or at least to influence action, through their writings. They felt unable to put public policy questions aside for further thought when politicians, leaders of multinational corporations, and others urgently demanded recommendations and remedies. In response, a whole generation of American intellectuals adopted the populistic "can do" attitude that was firmly fixed in American political culture by survival in the wilderness during colonial days and by the opening and settling of the west during the nineteenth century.

When it was implanted among the postwar generation of young people who came of age as students during the 1960s, this "can do" stance reinforced the more visionary tendencies that had always been part of American political thought. The result was a wave of intense idealism that washed through American universities and the larger society over the next twenty years and that remains a marked aspect of university student bodies today. Younger academics and students urged participatory and egalitarian reforms of all kinds. Any fear that such reforms violated the limits of what is possible realistically in a complex postindustrial society like America and that might, therefore, be futile or even counterproductive was dismissed out of hand. Instead of designating a skeptical, cautious position in political discussion, "elites," "elitists," and "the WASP establishment" became favorite pejoratives, used at once to denigrate privilege in all its forms and castigate those who denied privilege to the many students and others who, their egalitarian and participatory democratic rhetoric to the contrary notwithstanding, sought privileged statuses for themselves.

PROFESSIONAL AMERICAN POLITICAL THOUGHT

Professional American political thought was established as a distinct academic discipline in the older and more prestigious universities by the end of World War I. The complexities of American political institutions—federalism, the multiplicity of elective offices at state and local levels, the power of courts, the quasi-monarchical presidency—led many students to undertake formal studies in "government" departments at that time and subsequently. Because the principal aim of those departments was to enlighten and better enable citizens to participate in America's complex political institutions, their teaching and research content was highly factual and little shaped by philosophical and moral questions. In such methodological considerations as the new discipline harbored, it was basically historical; indeed, most government departments had emerged through the division of history departments. Thirty years later, after the end of World War II, practically all larger universities and colleges had what were usually called political science departments devoted to the professional study of politics and public administration.

In the new global circumstances of the United States after 1945, many political scientists became deeply concerned about their discipline's methodological foundations. Part of their concern stemmed from the fact that the public in general and most governmental and private bureaucracies did not regard political science as a vocational specialization analogous to the natural sciences or even economics. Persons trained in political science therefore had no special claim to employment. In addition, as part of the general engagement of intellectuals in political influence wielding and policymaking that came with the expansion of government domestically and with U.S. power internationally, political scientists worried that their discipline lacked any credible basis for proffering policy recommendations and providing firm answers to political questions.

Out of these concerns, a "behavioral" movement grew and began to take over the major graduate programs in political science from the mid-1950s. It was strongly pushed by some professors, especially those involved in advising government or who sought to influence policy through their writings as well as by a good many of their more ambitious students. The behavioral movement kept the discipline stirred up throughout the 1960s and 1970s. One of its major aspects was a stress on "empirical theory," that is, theory that dealt with strictly factual questions. Previously, "theory'" about political matters had referred to the ideas of philosophers, such as Plato and Aristotle, handed down over the ages. Although customarily taught in political science departments, those ideas had no clear relationship to the more factual aspects of politics. By contrast, "empirical theory" referred to something like the theories of chemists and physicists as these were explained in the philosophy of science literature. The development and application of political theories in a natural science sense seemed to be the behavioral movement's primary goal.

A second major aspect of the behavioral movement was recourse to various kinds of "objective" data and statistical techniques for uncovering and measuring the strength of relationships that might be embedded in such data. The data most suitable for this purpose tended to be demographic and opinion surveys of non-elite populations and voters. These data contained numbers of cases sufficient to meet the requirements of probability statistics, and they incorporated enough items or "variables" so that one could search for a range of relationships in them. The design, funding, collection, and analysis of data about non-elites quickly became the main practical endeavor of behavioral political science.

The accumulation of data about non-elites that can be manipulated statistically has been the behavioral movement's greatest influence on American political scientists. This is probably because quantitative research skills and techniques can more easily be developed and imparted to graduate students than can theories and substantive approaches, especially those involving considerable knowledge of history. The bulk of work and training in behavioral political science came to concentrate on the statistical analysis of numerical data, particularly political opinion polling and other survey data, using ever more sophisticated statistical techniques. Prevailingly, American political scientists investigated questions amenable to polling and survey research and to quantitative statements about them at a time when the real questions facing American political thought were largely devoid of elements that could be treated in that way.

In particular, the behavioral movement was reluctant to embrace theories that depended for their operation on essentially unmeasurable and contingent workings of key entities like elites and their choices and actions. It is difficult to avoid concluding that this has been why behavioral empirical theories contributed rather little to the understanding of major political changes and continuities in the contemporary world. The harvest of knowledge since the behavioral movement came to dominate professional political thought might have been greater if theories had more often been related to imponderables and contingencies in politics than to investigating non-elite preferences and proclivities with the use of multivariate models and statistical techniques.

POLITICAL THOUGHT CONFOUNDED

Looking back at the period since World War II, the major political changes of those seven decades have tended to surprise, confound, and baffle American political scientists and other observers of politics at nearly every turn. No sooner was an "end of ideology" thesis propounded in the late 1950s than left-wing radicalism of an especially vehement kind became one of the most striking features of the 1960s. No sooner were conformity and complacency proclaimed to be hallmarks of the postwar "status-seeking" society than a profusion of incongruous, frequently bizarre lifestyles and personal demeanors became conspicuous features of the landscape. No sooner was the welfare state extolled as a panacea for social ills than poverty of an especially intractable kind was found to be spreading and desolating many urban and rural areas, while indices of criminal behavior, narcotics addiction, suicide, and other mayhem pointing to a deepening social and political malaise increased (Wilensky 2002, 523–26, 767–69). Looking abroad, no sooner had scholars and statesmen persuaded themselves that a combination of American political example and foreign aid would soon enable "Third World" countries to emulate American political practices than authoritarian regimes became rampant in Latin America, Africa, and other world regions.

More recent changes have been similarly unforeseen: the sudden collapse of what were thought to be entrenched totalitarian regimes in the Soviet Union, Eastern Europe, and Yugoslavia; the rise of a New Right and its onslaught on the welfare state; the election to the presidency of a movie star and later a television star, both disinclined to serious political thought; a large and growing population of homeless people on the streets of American cities; a subsidence of democracy in numerous non-Western and some East European countries; and an upsurge of populist nationalism across the West.

The reaction of many educated Americans to these and similarly unforeseen developments has been mainly to reassert traditional populistic non-elite goals, often in extreme form. Thus, students and others demand, or sympathize with demands for, liberation from all customary political and social restraints and for compensatory advantages for women and minority groups to make them equal with everyone else. Sexual taboos and the authority of parents over children, of teachers over students, of governments over soldiers, of wardens over prisoners, and of police over rioters have come under strong attack. An insistence on "human rights" is thought to be the solvent of despotism in the wider world.

Although more sophisticated and experienced Americans have recognized practical reasons why such demands cannot soon be satisfied, there is a strong tendency to view practical considerations as necessary concessions to elite power or to perverse social habits such as systematic racism. Many Americans appear to believe that, while it might currently be inexpedient to enforce strict political and other forms of non-elite equality and human rights in the society and in the world, such traditional American goals remain serious possibilities that warrant earnest pursuit. Although tempered somewhat by the ascendancy of right-wing political forces since the 1980s that culminated in the Donald Trump presidency, these utopian outlooks remain part of the thinking of many who grew up when they were widely and unhesitatingly expressed and among their offspring today.

In sum, what stands out in a review of the decades since World War II is how frequently misguided or plainly wrong political analyses and forecasts of American and world political and social trends have been. Assumptions about the causal importance of non-elite populations in politics permeate American political thought and have been so grossly deficient when applied to actual trends and developments as to indicate a profound intellectual crisis. American political thought involves, quite simply, a near total inability to explain and predict political change with the stock of ideas and outlooks generated by American history. American political thinkers therefore find themselves in a situation calling for genuine and wholesale innovation, involving unfamiliar concepts, formulae, and evaluations along lines this book has explored.

Bibliography

Aylmer, George E. 1986. *Rebellion or Revolution? England from Civil War to Restoration.* London: Oxford University Press.

Bachrach, Peter. 1967. *The Theory of Democratic Elitism: A Critique.* Boston: Little, Brown.

Barany, Zoltan. 2011. "Comparing Arab Revolts: The Role of the Military." *Journal of Democracy* 22, no. 4 (October): 24–35.

Barone, Michael. 2007. *Our First Revolution: The Remarkable British Upheaval that Inspired America's Founding Fathers.* New York: Crown.

Bell, Daniel. 1973. *The Coming of Post-Industrial Society.* New York: Basic Books.

Bendix, Reinhard. 1978. *Kings or People: Power and the Mandate to Rule.* Berkeley: University of California Press.

Best, Heinrich, and John Higley, eds. 2010. *Democratic Elitism: New Theoretical and Comparative Perspectives.* Leiden: Brill.

Borchert, Jens, and Jürgen Zeiss, eds. 2003. *The Political Class in Advanced Democracies.* London: Oxford University Press.

Burton, Michael, and John Higley. 1987. "Elite Settlements." *American Sociological Review* 52 no. 3 (June): 295–307.

Brighton, Andrea, Werner Eichhorst, et al. 2015. "Precarious Employment in Europe." Report to the European Parliament, PE587.303.

Brinton, Crane. 1938. *The Anatomy of Revolution.* New York: Vintage.

Bürklin, Wilhelm, and Hilke Rebenstorf. 1997. *Eliten in Deutschland* [Elites in Germany]. Opladen: Leske and Budrich.

Case, Anne, and Angus Deacon. 2020. *Deaths of Despair and the Future of Capitalism.* Princeton, NJ: Princeton University Press.

Casselman, Ben. 2017. "Why Some Scars from the Recession May Never Vanish." *New York Times*, October 6.

Clark, Martin. 1984. *Modern Italy, 1871–1982*. New York: Longman.

Cohen, Roger. 2021. "France Battles Over Whether to Cancel or Celebrate Napoleon." *New York Times*, May 5, 2021, A13.

Cohn, Norman. 1961. *The Pursuit of the Millennium*. New York: Oxford University Press.

Colley, Linda. 2021. *The Gun, the Ship, and the Pen*. New York: Norton.

Cotta, Maurizio. 2014. "Facing the Crisis: The European Elite System's Changing Geometry." In *Political Elites in the Transatlantic Crisis*, edited by Heinrich Best and John Higley, 58–80. London: Palgrave Macmillan.

De Mesquita, Bruce Bueno, and George W. Downs. 2005. "Development and Democracy." *Foreign Affairs* 84 (September–October): 77–86.

Diamond, Larry. 2008. *The Spirit of Democracy: The Struggle to Build Free Societies Throughout the World*. New York: Holt, 2008.

Dogan, Mattei. 2003. "Is There a Ruling Class in France?" In *Elite Configurations at the Apex of Power*, edited by Mattei Dogan, 17–90. Amsterdam: Brill.

Draper, Theodore. 1965. *Castroism: Theory and Practice*. New York: Praeger.

Dye, Thomas R. 2014. *Who's Running America? The Obama Reign*. Boulder, CO: Paradigm Books.

Eberstadt, Nicolas. 2016. *Men Without Work. America's Invisible Crisis*. West Conoshocken, PA: Templeton.

Evans, Richard J. 2003. *The Coming of the Third Reich*. New York: Penguin.

Fairbank, John King. 1986. *The Great Chinese Revolution, 1800–1985*. New York: Harper and Row.

Femia, Joseph V. 2007. *Pareto and Political Theory*. London: Routledge.

Field, G. Lowell. 1967. *Comparative Political Development*. Ithaca, NY: Cornell University Press.

Field, G. Lowell, and John Higley. 1980. *Elitism*. London: Kegan and Paul.

Filkins, Dexter. 2021. "No Exit." *The New Yorker*, March 8, 42–49.

Finer, Samuel E. 1966. "Introduction." In *Vilfredo Pareto: Sociological Writings*, edited by Samuel E. Finer, 1–91. Tottawa, NJ: Rowman & Littlefield.

Frankel, Todd C. 2021. "A Majority of the People Arrested for Capitol Riot Had a History of Financial Trouble." *Washington Post*, February 10.

Fukuyama, Francis. 2012. "The Future of History." *Foreign Affairs* 91, no. 1: 53–61.

———. 2014. *Political Order and Political Decay*. New York: Farrar, Straus and Giroux.

Galbraith, John Kenneth. 1958. *The Affluent Society*. New York: Houghton Mifflin.

Gordon, Philip H. 2020. *Losing the Long Game: The False Promise of Regime Change in the Middle East*. New York: St. Martin's Press.

Gray, John. 2007. *Black Mass: Apocalyptic Religion and the Death of Utopia*. New York: Farrar, Straus and Giroux.

Gulbrandsen, Trygve, et al. 2002. *Norsk Makrteliter* [Norwegian Power Elites]. Oslo: Gyldendahl.

Gunther, Richard. 1992. "Spain: The Very Model of the Modern Elite Settlement." In *Elites and Democratic Consolidation in Latin America and Southern Europe*, edited by John Higley and Richard Gunther, 38–80. New York: Cambridge University Press.

Hamilton, Richard F. 1982. *Who Voted for Hitler?* Princeton, NJ: Princeton University Press.

Hart, John Mason. 1987. *Revolutionary Mexico: The Coming and Process of the Mexican Revolution*. Berkeley: University of California Press.

Higley, John. 2016. *The Endangered West: Myopic Elites and Fragile Social Orders in a Threatening World*. New York: Routledge.

Higley, John, and Michael Burton. 2006. *Elite Foundations of Liberal Democracy*. Lanham, MD: Rowman & Littlefield.

Higley, John, and Richard Gunther, eds. 1992. *Elites and Democratic Consolidation in Latin America and Southern Europe*. New York: Cambridge University Press.

Huntington, Samuel P. 1991. *The Third Wave*. Norman: University of Oklahoma Press.

———. 1996. *The Clash of Civilizations*. New York: Simon and Schuster.

Keller, Suzanne. 1963. *Beyond the Ruling Class: Strategic Elites in Modern Society*. New York: Random House.

Klansjek, Rudi, and Sergej Flere. 2019. *The Rise and Fall of Socialist Yugoslavia*. Lanham, MD: Lexington Books.

Knight, Alan. 1986. *The Mexican Revolution*. 2 vols. New York: Cambridge University Press.

———. 1992. "Mexico's Elite Settlement: Conjuncture and Consequences." In *Elites and Democratic Consolidation in Latin America and Southern Europe*, edited by John Higley and Richard Gunther, 113–45. New York: Cambridge University Press.

Kurlantzick, Joshua. 2013. *Democracy in Retreat: The Revolt of the Middle Class and the Worldwide Decline of Representative Government*. New Haven, CT: Yale University Press.

Lachmann, Richard. 1987. *From Manor to Market: Structural Change in England, 1536–1640*. Madison: University of Wisconsin Press.

———. 1989. "Elite Conflict and State Formation in 16th and 17th-Century England and France." *American Sociological Review* 54, no. 2 (April): 141–62.

Lengyel, György, and Gabriella Ilonszki. 2016. "The Illiberal Turn in Hungary: Institutions and Leadership." In *The Visegrad Countries in Crisis*, edited by Jan Pakulski, 27–45. Warsaw: Collegium Civitas.

Li, Cheng. 2018. "The Political Elite in China: A Dynamic Between Integration and Differentiation." In *The Palgrave Handbook of Political Elites*, edited by Heinrich Best and John Higley, 295–314. London: Palgrave Macmillan.

Lindsay, Michael. 2014. *View from the Top*. New York: Wiley.

Linz, Juan J., and Alfred Stepan, eds. 1978. *The Breakdown of Democratic Regimes: Vol. 2: Europe*. Baltimore, MD: Johns Hopkins University Press.

———. 1996. *Problems of Democratic Transition and Consolidation*. Baltimore, MD: Johns Hopkins University Press.

Macfarquhar, Roderick, and Michael Schoenhals. 2006. *Mao's Last Revolution*. Boston: The Belknap Press of Harvard University Press.

MBO Partners. 2015. *The New American Workforce: Flying Solo Feels Safer*. Herndon, VA: MBO Partners, Inc.

Merritt, Richard L. 1970. *Systematic Approaches to Comparative Politics*. Chicago: Rand McNally.

Michels, Robert. 2015/1962. *Political Parties: A Sociological Study of the Oligarchical Tendencies of Modern Democracy*. New York: Collier Books.

Mishra, Pankaj. 2021. "Struggle Sessions." *The New Yorker*, February 1, 61–65.

Monck, Peter, Birgit Möller, and Lise Togeby. 2001. *Den danske elite* [The Danish Elite]. Copenhagen: Hans Reitzels Forlag.

Moore, Barrington, Jr. 1966. *Social Origins of Dictatorship and Democracy: Lord and Peasant in the Making of the Modern World*. Boston: Beacon Press.

Mounk, Yascha. 2018. *The People vs. Democracy*. Cambridge, MA: Harvard University Press.

———. 2021. "Democracy on the Defense." *Foreign Affairs* 100, no. 2: 163–73.

Mudde, Cas. 2004. "The Populist Zeitgeist." *Government and Opposition* 39, no. 4: 541–63.

———. 2018. "Populism in the Twenty-First Century: An Illiberal Response to Undemocratic Liberalism." Accessed March 4, 2018. https://www.sas.upenn.edu/andrea-mitchell-center/cas-midde-populism-twenty-firstcentury.

Mudde, Cas, and Cristobal Rovira Kaltwasser. 2017. *Populism: A Very Short Introduction*. Oxford: Oxford University Press.

Murray, Charles. 2012. *Coming Apart: The State of White America, 1960–2010*. New York: Crown Forum.

Müller, Jan-Werner. 2016. *What Is Populism?* New York: Penguin.

Packer, George. 2013. *The Unwinding: An Inner History of the New America*. New York: Farrar, Straus and Giroux.

Pakulski, Jan. 2016. "Crumbling Elite Consensus and the Illiberal Turn in Poland." In *The Visegrad Countries in Crisis*, edited by Jan Pakulski, 47–62. Warsaw: Collegium Civitas.

Pareto, Vilfredo. 1916/1935. *The Mind and Society: A Treatise on General Sociology*. Translated by Andrew Bongiorno and Arthur Livingston. New York: Dover.

Paxton, Robert O. 2004. *The Anatomy of Fascism*. New York: Knopf.

Plumb, John H. 1967. *The Growth of Political Stability in England, 1675–1725*. London: Macmillan.

Putnam, Robert D. 2000. *Bowling Alone*. New York: Simon and Schuster.

———. 2015. *Our Kids: The American Dream in Crisis*. New York: Simon and Schuster.

Ricks, Thomas. 2006. *Fiasco: The American Military Adventure in Iraq*. New York: Penguin.

Rucker, Philip, and Carol Leonnig. 2020. *A Very Stable Genius: Donald J. Trump's Testing of America*. New York: Random House.

Rustow, Dankwart. 1970. "Transitions to Democracy: Toward a Dynamic Model." *Comparative Politics* 2: 337–63.

Sartori, Giovanni. 1987. *The Theory of Democracy Revisited: Vol. 1: The Contemporary Debate*. Chatham, NJ: Chatham House Books.

Schama, Simon. 1989. *Citizens: A Chronicle of the French Revolution*. New York: Knopf.

Schumpeter, Joseph. 1942. *Capitalism, Socialism, and Democracy*. New York: Harper and Row.

Skocpol, Theda. 1979. *States and Social Revolution: A Comparative Analysis of France, Russia, and China*. New York: Cambridge University Press.

Snyder, Timothy. 2017. *On Tyranny: Twenty Lessons from the Twentieth Century*. New York: Tim Duggan Books.

Tilly, Charles. 1978. *From Mobilization to Revolution*. New York: Random House.

Thompson, Edward P. 1963. *The Making of the British Working Class*. London: Victor Gollanz.

Thompson, Mark. 2008. *The White War: Life and Death on the Italian Front, 1915–1919*. London: Faber and Faber.

Turchin, Peter. 2016. *Ages of Discord. A Structural-Demographic Analysis of American History*. Chaplin, CT: Beresta Books.

Tyson, Laura, and Susan Lund. 2021. "The Post-Pandemic Labor Market's Long-Term Scars." *Project Syndicate*, March 17. https://prosyn.org/cBX6RV8.

U.S. Department of State. 2021. "A Foreign Policy for the American People." Speech by Secretary of State Anthony Blinkin, March 3.

Volpe, Giorgio. 2021. *Italian Elitism and the Reshaping of Democracy in the United States.* New York: Routledge.

Weiner, Myron F. 1987. *Competitive Elections in Developing Countries.* Durham, NC: Duke University Press.

Wilensky, Harold L. 2002. *Rich Democracies: Political Economy, Public Policy, and Performance.* Berkeley: University of California Press.

Wilson, Julius. 1997. *When Work Disappears: The New World of the Urban Poor.* New York: Viking.

Winters, Jeffrey. 2011. *Oligarchy.* New York: Cambridge.

Woodward, Bob. 2018. *Fear: Trump in the White House.* New York: Simon and Schuster.

Yang, Jisheng. 2016/2021. *The World Turned Upside Down: A History of the Chinese Cultural Revolution.* Translated by Stacey Moser and Guo Jian. New York: Farrar, Straus and Giroux.

Zaret, David. 1989. "Religion and the Rise of Liberal Democratic Ideology in 17th-Century England." *American Sociological Review* 54, no. 2: 163–79.

Index

Walesa, Lech, 86
Washington, George, 92
Weimar Republic, 51, 54–55
welfare programs, xi–xii, 74,
 137–38; middle-class opinion
 of, 11
Western countries, ix–x, 123–24;
 authoritarian regimes tracked
 by, 70–71; democratization led
 by political leaders of, 69–71;
 dominance of, 115–19; elites
 in, 74, 122; ideology in, 67;
 liberalism in, 89–90, 97–98;
 meritocracy in, 120–21; political
 ideals in non-western and, 71–72,
 113–29; student radicalism in
 1960s, 68–69
Whigs, 13; Tories *vs.*, 47
Who's Running America? (Rye), 6
Wilhelm II (Kaiser), 51
William the Silent, 92
women: of Afghanistan, 123;
 unemployment and, 77–78
work: insecurity of, 77, 124;
 postindustrialization and
 insecurity of, 80–81; role of,
 in preindustrialization and
 postindustrialization, 32–33
workers, 113–14; autonomy of,
 21; clash of economic interests
 and political orientations of, 76;
 during industrialization, 34–35;
 relationship to supervisor, 22
workers, artisan and agricultural:
 decrease of, 75; during
 industrialization, 24–25; during
 preindustrialization, 24; material
 environment of, 21; relationship
 to power, 23–24, 25
workers, manual industrial, 21;
 alienation of, 29; decrease of,

75; during preindustrialization,
 25–26; egalitarianism of, 26
workers, nonmanual bureaucratic
 and service: class and, 30; during
 industrialization, 27–30; during
 postindustrialization, 30; elites
 and non-elites as, 28–30; increase
 of, 75; leisure and influence for,
 29; social environment of, 21–22
workforce: expansion of Western,
 27; of postindustrialization, and
 socioeconomic development, 31;
 shrinking of, 77–78
workforce components, 29–30;
 in different socioeconomic
 development stages, 34; modal
 sizes of, during modern history,
 23; in postindustrialization, 56–57
working-class, 31; culture replacing
 rural, 26; demoralization
 among, 78–79; mobilized by
 industrialization, 50; revolts in
 northern Italy (1921-1922), 55
World War I, 9, 49, 58, 135;
 ideological unified elite during,
 49–50; Italy and Germany
 after, 53
World War II, 9, 15, 19, 91, 97,
 114; Japan post-WWII, 17; living
 standards post-WWII, 119; New
 Deal and, 133–34; optimism post-
 WWII, 119–20; political science
 after, 135–39

Yugoslavia, elites of, 19–20

Zapata, Emiliano, 42–43, 48
Zapatistas, 45
Zinoviev, Grigory, 53